Sofia Bompiani

# A Short History of the Italian Waldenses

Who Have Inhabited the Valleys of the Cottian Alps

Sofia Bompiani

**A Short History of the Italian Waldenses**
*Who Have Inhabited the Valleys of the Cottian Alps*

ISBN/EAN: 9783743418639

Manufactured in Europe, USA, Canada, Australia, Japa

Cover: Foto ©ninafisch / pixelio.de

Manufactured and distributed by brebook publishing software (www.brebook.com)

Sofia Bompiani

**A Short History of the Italian Waldenses**

# A SHORT HISTORY

OF

# THE ITALIAN WALDENSES

MAP OF THE WALDENSIAN VALLEYS; THE CHURCHES
AND STATIONS OF THE MISSION.

A SHORT HISTORY

OF

# The Italian Waldenses

WHO HAVE INHABITED THE VALLEYS
OF THE COTTIAN ALPS

From Ancient Times to the Present

BY

SOPHIA V. BOMPIANI

AUTHOR OF "ITALIAN EXPLORERS IN AFRICA"

NEW YORK
A. S. BARNES AND COMPANY
LONDON: HODDER & STOUGHTON
1897

**University Press**
JOHN WILSON AND SON, CAMBRIDGE, U.S.A.

# PREFACE.

THE present generation of Italian Waldenses, with that firmness characteristic of the race, believe that their forefathers lived in the Valleys of the Cottian Alps from "time immemorial." Without documents to prove their existence as evangelical Christians in these Valleys previous to the time of Peter Waldo in the twelfth century, they yet obstinately reject the theory that he was their founder. They pay him no especial honor as do Lutherans to Luther; Wesleyans to Wesley; Calvinists to Calvin; Mahometans to Mahomet; Buddhists to Buddha.

Unable to prove these traditions of their more ancient origin, they listen with respect, but without assent, to the documented histories of their race, dating from Peter Waldo, written by some of their most learned professors. In

## Preface

truth there is little to say against these conclusions except the traditions and convictions of an ancient race fixed for centuries in the same locality, and the rare traces of them found in the writings of their enemies. These few arguments found in the writings of other historians of the Waldenses I have gathered for this modest little work.

S. B.

ROME, ITALY, 1897.

# CONTENTS.

| Chapter | | Page |
|---|---|---|
| I. | The Israel of the Alps | 1 |
| II. | The Diocese of Bishop Claudio of Turin in the Ninth Century | 12 |
| III. | Who were the Albigenses? | 20 |
| IV. | Antiquity of the Waldenses before Peter Waldo | 25 |
| V. | The "Noble Lesson" | 32 |
| VI. | Calumnies and Oppressions of the Inquisitors | 40 |
| VII. | Geographical Position and Colonies | 48 |
| VIII. | The Ministers, or "Barbes" | 55 |
| IX. | Persecution begun in the Year 1476 | 63 |
| X. | Persecution of A.D. 1561 | 70 |
| XI. | Persecution of Easter, 1655 | 78 |
| XII. | The Glorious Return in 1689 | 86 |
| XIII. | Extirpation of the Colony in Calabria | 94 |
| XIV. | Language changed after the Pest in 1630 | 102 |
| XV. | Heroes | 111 |

## Contents

| Chapter | | Page |
|---|---|---|
| XVI. | Martyrs | 120 |
| XVII. | Women | 130 |
| XVIII. | Friends — General Beckwith | 140 |
| XIX. | Emancipation in 1848 | 148 |
| XX. | A.D. 1889. — Bi-Centenary of "Glorious Return" | 156 |

# LIST OF ILLUSTRATIONS.

MAP OF THE WALDENSIAN VALLEYS; THE CHURCHES
    AND STATIONS OF THE MISSION . . . *Frontispiece*
TORRE PELLICE, THE CAPITAL OF THE VALLEYS *To face p.* 5
ENTRANCE TO TORRE PELLICE, ROMAN CATHOLIC
    CHURCH . . . . . . . . . . . . . . . 15
WALDENSIAN CHURCH AT SAN GIOVANNI . . . . 23
CASCADE OF THE PIS AT MASSELLO . . . . . . 57
SCHOOL OF THE BARBES AT PRÀ DEL TORNO, AN-
    GROGNA . . . . . . . . . . . . . . . 57
WALDENSIAN CHURCH AT ANGROGNA . . . . . 63
FROM ANGROGNA TO PRÀ DEL TORNO . . . . . 67
ANGROGNA . . . . . . . . . . . . . . . . 75
ROUTE OF RETURN OF WALDENSIAN PEOPLE FROM
    SWITZERLAND THROUGH SAVOY . . . . . . 87
PORTRAIT OF CATINAT . . . . . . . . . . . 89
PORTRAIT OF HENRI ARNAUD . . . . . . . . 91
PORTRAIT OF VICTOR AMEDEUS, DUKE OF SAVOY
    AND PRINCE OF PIEDMONT . . . . . . . . 93
      From an engraving by De l'Amerssini, published in Paris, 1684.
PRANGINS, LAKE LEMAN, FROM A PRINT . . . . 115
SIEGE OF BALSIGLIA, FROM AN OLD PRINT . . . . 157
WALDENSIAN RESIDENCE AND MUSEUM . . . . . 159
BADGES . . . . . . . . . . . . . . . . . 159

# A SHORT HISTORY

OF THE

# ITALIAN WALDENSES

## CHAPTER I

### THE ISRAEL OF THE ALPS

IN the valleys of the Cottian Alps, between Mount Cenis and Mount Viso, a Bible-loving people have lived from "time immemorial." They have been persecuted and exiled by the Bible-hating power which has its seat in Rome; but after exile they returned to their green valleys, and after persecution they were not destroyed. Now, like a healthy vine which has its roots in those valleys, the branches of this primitive Church spread out over all the Italian peninsula.

It has churches in all the great cities,— in Turin, Milan, Venice, Florence, Genoa, Rome, Naples, Palermo, Messina, and even at Vittoria, a small town at the extremity of Sicily. It has forty-four pastors and fifty-four hundred members in the mission churches of the peninsula, and twenty-two pastors and thirteen thousand five hundred members in the valleys. This hath God wrought for the Waldenses. They "kept the faith so pure of old," spite of torture, cold, destitution, and loss of life on the Alpine mountains. They were burned; they were cast into damp and horrid dungeons; they were smothered in crowds in mountain caverns, — mothers and babes, and old men and women together; they were sent out into exile of a winter night, unclothed and unfed, to climb the snowy mountains; they were hurled over the rocks; their heads were used as footballs; their houses and lands were taken from them, and their little children were stolen to be educated in the religion they abhorred. Yet they refused to acknowledge the Roman pontiff as the Vicar of Christ; to bow down to the wafer and believe it the body of Christ; to confess to priests, or to give up the Bible.

Long before the German Reformation they were an evangelical people, loving the Bible above all things: making translations of it into the vulgar tongue; spreading it abroad in Bohemia, in Germany, in France and in Italy. They taught their children to memorize whole chapters, so that whatever might befall the written copies of the Bible, large portions of it might be secure in the memories of their youths and maidens. In secret meetings, when they went by night barefooted, or with shoes bound with rags, so that they might not be heard in passing, it was their custom to listen to the Gospels recited in turn by the young, each one responsible for a certain portion.

In spite of all their sorrows, often occasioned by the weakness or bigotry of the dukes and duchesses of Savoy, of whom they were the subjects, the Waldenses never failed in patriotic love and service to their country.

They are and always have been Italians, but were often driven by the persecutions of the middle ages into the French valleys, where they found brethren of the same faith, and learned their language. Beaten about like the waves of the sea, backward and forward, they had no rest. At one time thirteen out of fifteen of their pastors died of the plague, and they were obliged to send to Geneva for French pastors, who introduced the French language into the valleys. Their prince, Victor Amedeus II., Duke of Savoy, urged to do so by Louis XIV. of France, and by the

Pope, drove them with cruel persecution into Switzerland.

Yet, when the tide changed, and they by an heroic march had returned, — when he had need of them to guard the Alps against the inroads of that same Louis XIV. who had persuaded him to drive them away, — they gave him true and loyal service. Until the year 1848 they were shut up in their mountains without civil rights, — the very pariahs and outcasts of Italy. A Waldensian could not exercise a learned profession, or take a regular course of study in the universities of Italy, or worship according to his faith outside of the valleys. Yet they were ever ready to greet their princes with respect and fealty on the rare visits made them, and no Italians have been more faithful to the established government since their admission by the *statuto* to equal civil and religious rights with other citizens. Fervent prayers are sent up every Sunday to the throne of grace from every Waldensian pulpit in Italy for the welfare of "King Humbert, Queen Margaret, Victor Emanuel Ferdinand, Prince of Naples; for the Senate, the Parliament, and all others in authority."

No trace of bitterness or revenge is evident

TORRE PELLICE, THE CAPITOL OF THE VALLEY.

against those who once persecuted their race to the death. But yet they are faithful to the oath taken two hundred years ago at Sibaud, in the valleys, when, on their return from three years and a half of exile, they swore to drag their fellow-countrymen away by every means in their power from the Babylonian woe. This missionary spirit has possessed them always.

Their pastors or barbes went, two by two, dressed in long brown woollen gowns, over all Italy to evangelize in the thirteenth, fourteenth, and fifteenth centuries. They had churches and adherents in every town and city, and were always the guests of their own people.

With the dawn of liberty in 1848, they awoke to new missionary life and vigor. Churches and stations were established, and a committee of five pastors was appointed to collect money from Protestant Christians in other countries. Seventy thousand dollars are now needed annually for the wants of the mission churches. All this must be collected little by little, — a heavy task for those who engage in the arduous work. The Waldenses own their church buildings in the principal cities. The beautiful edifice on the Via

Nazionale, in Rome, dedicated in the year 1885, is built on a foundation of gray granite brought from the valleys.

The very rocks that were often bathed in the blood of maidens and babes and old men, — innocent or conscious martyrs to their faith, — now rest on the soil of persecuting Rome, and support that building which is the ever-present witness to the goodness of God to his people.

The origin of the Waldenses is lost in the night of centuries. Their traditions assert that they were driven from southern Italy, in the time of the second and third centuries, to the Alpine valleys, where they have ever since lived. But they possess no written evidence of this antiquity, and only believe it because from time to time, from one generation to another, their forefathers have constantly asserted it. The profound conviction of an entire race, with few exceptions, may well be considered valuable, even in the absence of written documents. Of these they have none previous to the year 1100, when the "Noble Lesson" was written. But many arguments in favor of their early Christian origin exist which are found chiefly in the voluminous writings in Latin left by their enemies.

There, amidst many calumnies and false representations, are found, like pearls in the mud, the confessions of faith of the martyrs and the claims they made for the antiquity and purity of their Church. An Inquisitor, Reinerius Sacco, in the thirteenth century, calling them the "Leonists," said: "There is not one of the sects of ancient heretics more pernicious to the Church than that of the Leonists; first, because it has been of longer continuance, for some say it has lasted from the time of Pope Sylvester, others from the time of the apostles; second, because it is more diffused, for there is scarcely any land in which this sect exists not; and third, because the Leonists have a great semblance of piety, inasmuch as they live justly before men, and believe, together with all the doctrines contained in the creed, every point respecting the Deity. But they blaspheme the Roman Church and clergy."

Another writer of the thirteenth century says that "the people who claimed to have existed from the time of Pope Sylvester were the Waldenses;" while Claude Seyssel, Archbishop of Turin in the sixteenth century, says that "the Valdenses of Piedmont derived from a person named Leo, who, in the time of the Emperor Constantine, execrating the avarice of Pope Sylvester and the immoderate endowment of the Roman Church, seceded from that communion, and drew after him all those who entertained the same ideas."

The Waldenses, or Valdenses, or Vaudois, — men of the valleys, or dalesmen, — and the Leonists are therefore the same.

Long before the time of Peter the Waldo of Lyons, they bore the name of Leonists from one of their teachers, named Leo. But even he is not considered their founder, and some of the present Waldenses believe their origin is in a direct, unbroken line from the primitive Christians.

This traditional Leo of the Waldenses is no other than the famous Vigilantius Leo, or Vigilantius, the Leonist of Lyons, in Aquitaine, upon the borders of the Pyrenees, and a presbyter of the church of Barcelona in Spain. This holy man charged Jerome with too great a leaning to the opinions of Origen, and wrote a treatise against the celibacy of the clergy; the excessive veneration of the martyrs and blind reverence of their relics; the boasted sanctity of monasticism and pilgrimages to Jerusalem or other sanctuaries. This work of Vigilantius Leo has been lost, but the violent answer made to it by Jerome still exists. "I have seen," says Jerome, "that monster called Vigilantius. I tried by quoting passages of Scripture to enchain that infuriated one; but he is gone; he has escaped to that region where King Cottius reigned, between the Alps and the waves of the Adriatic. From thence he has cried out against me, and, ah, wickedness! there he has found bishops who share his crime."

This region, where King Cottius reigned, once a part of Cisalpine Gaul, is the precise country of the Waldenses. Here Leo, or Vigilantius, retired for safety from persecution, among a people already established there of his own way of thinking, who received him as a brother, and who thenceforth for several centuries were sometimes called by his name. Here, shut up in the Alpine valleys, they handed down through the generations the doctrines and practices of the primitive Church, while the inhabitants of the plains of Italy were daily sinking more and more into the apostasy foretold by the Apostles.

The hero of the glorious return from exile in 1689, Colonel Henri Arnaud, who led nine hundred Waldenses over the Alps to their homes, writes: "The Vaudois are descendants of those refugees from southern Italy, who, after St. Paul had there preached the gospel, were persecuted, and abandoned their beautiful country; fleeing like the woman mentioned in the Apocalypse, to these wild mountains, where they have to this day handed down the gospel from father to son in the same purity and simplicity as it was preached by St. Paul."

The confession which they presented, A.D. 1544, to the French king, Francis I., said: "This is that confession which we have received from our ancestors, even from hand to hand, according as their predecessors in all times and in every age have taught and delivered."

And in the year 1559, in their supplication to Emanuel Philibert of Savoy, they say: "Let your highness consider that this religion in which we live is not merely our religion of the present day, but it is the religion of our fathers and of our grandfathers, yea, of our forefathers and of our predecessors still more remote. It is the religion of the saints and of the martyrs, of the confessors and of the Apostles." When addressing the German Reformers of the sixteenth century, they say: "Our ancestors have often recounted to us that we have existed from the time of the

Apostles." They agreed with the Reformers in all points of doctrine, but refused to be called a Reformed Church, as they said they had never swerved from the true Christian faith, and needed no reformation.

# CHAPTER II

### THE DIOCESE OF BISHOP CLAUDIO OF TURIN IN THE NINTH CENTURY

THE Waldenses are known to have existed in the ninth century in the valleys of the Cottian Alps. The evidence of this must have been clear to their enemy, Rorenco, prior of St. Rock, at Turin, who in 1630 studied the history of the "Heresies of the Valleys." He owns that "the Waldenses were so ancient as to afford no certainty in regard to the time of their origin, but that in the ninth century they were rather to be deemed a race of fomenters and encouragers of opinions which had preceded them."

Dungal, an ecclesiastic, who was the bitter enemy of Claude, Bishop of Turin in the year 820, said that the people of Claude's diocese were divided into two parts "concerning the images and the holy pictures of the Lord's passion; the Catholics saying that that picture is good and useful, and almost as profitable as Holy Scripture itself, and the heretics, on the contrary, saying that it is a seduction into error, and no other than idolatry."

Dungal makes constant reference to Vigilantius, and charges Claude and his Vallenses with teaching the same doctrines as the Leonist. Vigilantius, he said, was the neighbor and spiritual ancestor of Claude, — both being natives of Spain, — and the author of "his madness."

But this was a holy madness, which they both learned from Scripture and from the primitive Church. The writings of Dungal prove that after a lapse of four centuries the memory and influence of Vigilantius remained among the men of the valleys, and that, although the faithful preaching of Claude encouraged and strengthened their faith, they did not owe to him its origin.

Claude was the court chaplain of Louis the Meek, the son of Charlemagne. He was appointed by that Emperor, Bishop of Turin, which city he found "full of images." "When, sorely against my will," he says, "I undertook, at the command of Louis the Pious, the burden of a Bishoprick, I found all the churches of Turin stuffed full of vile and accursed images." He alone began to destroy what all were "sottishly worshipping," and had the Lord not helped him they would have swallowed him up quick. He became a reproach to some of his neighbors, but God, the Father of Mercies, comforted him in all his afflictions, so that he might comfort others who "were weighed down with sorrow." These "others" were the partakers of his affliction, kindred souls, objects like himself of scorn and hate; the successors of those whom Jerome vituperated, inhabiting the mountain valleys in the diocese of Turin.

Turin was "wholly given to idolatry," but the Valdenses held firmly with their Bishop the doctrines of the Gospel. They, with him, rejected image worship, and saint worship, and bone and ash worship, and cross worship, and pilgrimages to Rome, and papal supremacy. "All these things," said Claude, "are mighty ridiculous." He continued to combat error and keep the Church committed to him free from idolatrous rites and anti-Christian dogmas, teaching no new doctrine, but keeping to the pure truth, and opposing to the uttermost all superstitions. "I repress sects," he said,—his definition of a sect being any departure from the truth of Scripture. His sermons are models of simplicity and truth. "Why do you prostrate yourselves

ENTRANCE TO TORRE PELLICE.
Roman Catholic Church.

## The Diocese of Bishop Claudio 15

before images? Bow not down to them, for God made you erect, with the face towards heaven and towards Him. Look up there! Seek God above and lift up your heart to Him."

Claude wrote commentaries on the Epistles, on Genesis, Leviticus and Matthew. Some of the manuscripts still exist; one in the Abbey of Fleury, near Orleans; one in the library of St. Remi at Rheims, and one in England. The only one ever printed was the Commentary on the Epistle to the Galatians, nearly all the copies of which were destroyed by his enemies. But fragments of his works have been preserved in the manuscripts of his opponent and former friend, Jonas of Orleans, who thus unconsciously rendered him a service.

Jonas, while himself believing in the adoration of the cross, quotes these words of Claude against it, — "Nothing pleases them in our Lord but what delighted even the impious, the opprobrium of His passion, and the ignominy of His death. Why not, then, adore the cradle, the manger, the ship, the crown of thorns, the spike, the lance? God commands one thing, those men another. God commands to bear the cross, not to adore it. To serve God in this manner is to forsake Him."

The opposition of Claude and a part of his diocese to the worship of images was sustained, in the year 794, by the Council of Frankfort, when Charlemagne was present, and in 826 by the Council of Paris. But his enemies in Turin persecuted and reviled him. Dungal calls him "a mad blasphemer" and "a hissing serpent," for his "error" in opposing all kinds of image-worship. And Claude used no less vigorous language, for, being called to appear before a synod of bishops to answer for his conduct in banishing images from the churches, he refused on the ground that they were *congregatio asinorum*.

The bishop who girded the sword over his white surplice to fight the Saracen in that period of Moslem invasion might be expected to give such a sturdy answer as this.

Claude sealed his faith by martyrdom in the year 839, after having for many years courageously battled with his enemies. From that date the Valdenses were without a bishop, and confined as a race to the narrow limits of the valleys. The church of Jesus Christ and the Apostles shrank away from the errors of the Roman Church, and retired into the "wilderness," where it remained imprisoned for centuries. God sealed it up there for the day

## The Diocese of Bishop Claudio

of tribulation, when He tried it like as gold is tried in the refiner's fire. In all the plains of Lombardy the voice of truth was silenced. There, from the fourth to the ninth century, many had professed the early Christian faith in its purity. The Waldensian Church is believed to have extended its influence from Turin to Milan, as in all its existence it has been possessed by the missionary spirit.

Ambrose, Bishop of Milan, who died in the year 397, was called "the Rock of the Church," on account of his reverence for the Scriptures and opposition to all idolatrous practices. Another bishop of Milan, in the ninth century, "rejoiced in the goodness of God, which had raised up Claude, a true Christian champion."

The ancient emblem of the Waldensian church is a candlestick with the motto, — *Lux lucet in tenebris.* A candlestick in the oriental imagery of the Bible is a Church, and this Church had power from God to prophesy in sackcloth and ashes twelve hundred and sixty days or symbolic years. "Lo, I am with you always," Christ said to His Church before leaving it, promising to keep it in life and in purity until his return. No other Church calling itself Christian can claim to have had through all these centuries the spiritual presence of our Lord. Like a good olive tree it has borne abundant fruit of martyrs; like a faithful prophet it has testified against the idolatry and corruption of the Roman Church; like a light shining in a dark place, it has spread the gospel abroad.

But two witnesses were to prophesy so long in sorrow; *two* olive trees and two candlesticks were to stand before God on the earth, and were not these the Waldenses and the Albigenses? The true title of the Church situated in the valleys of Piedmont is the "Church of the united Vallenses and Albigenses." Persecuted for their doctrines, similar to those of the Waldenses, the Albigenses of France fled at different times, from 1165 to 1405 A.D., to the Alps for refuge. Welcomed by their friends, the Waldenses, who had been in those mountains from "time immemorial," they lived together for several centuries in amity, but keeping their separate names and organizations. Then, tried by a series of horrible persecutions, the two suffering churches united like two drops of rain, and were henceforth known under one name. From this time the name of the Albigenses is lost, but the memory of their sufferings in the persecutions of the thirteenth century, made by Pope Innocent III., survived in the hearts of their descendants. War was made, and regular armies were enrolled against them, until, slaughtered and routed, despoiled of property and dignities, they fled in every direction. The poor remnant which escaped from the racks and fires of the Inquisitors and Crusaders to the Alps preserved there, at least, its doctrines and its existence. The victims of these persecutions were innumerable, as, according to the Inquisitors, almost the whole population of that part of France was "infected with heresy." The "blessed Dominic," founder of the order of preachers which exists to this day, that "glorious servant of God," who, together with Simon de Montfort, directed this crusade, was canonized for his services, and admitted to the order of celestial nobility by Pope Gregory IX. Miraculous fragrance issued from the open sepulchre of this Beatus Domenicus, and he was seen by a prior translated to heaven, which opened to receive him.

# CHAPTER III

### WHO WERE THE ALBIGENSES?

WHO were these Albigenses, so numerous in Provence, Aquitaine, Languedoc, Gascony, and Dauphiny, a century before these terrible crusades and also before the conversion of Peter Waldo of Lyons? They called themselves Good Men or Apostolicals, and were called by their enemies Paulicians, Cathari, Petrobrusians, Henricians, Manicheans, Bulgarians, Paterines, Publicans, and in 1176 Albigenses, from the town of Albi, where they held a synod. They first were noticed in the south of France about the commencement of the eleventh century; but long before that a purer system of religion than that of Rome prevailed among the people there.

"This whole district of Toulouse," says a monk who wrote the history of this heretical region, "has ever been notorious for the detestable prevalence of this heretical pravity. Generation after generation, from father to son, the venom of superstitious infidelity has been successively diffused. O Toulouse! mother of heretics! O tabernacle of robbers!"

Still the opposition to Rome took no compact form, and showed itself chiefly in the preaching of eminent individuals against the worship of saints and images and relics, until, at the beginning of the eleventh century, appeared among this people, already prepared to resist papal authority, a well-disciplined handful of strangers from the East. These Paulicians or Cathari were only four thousand, but they formed a rallying point to resist the tyranny of Rome, and the number of their local proselytes, called Believers, was soon innumerable.

The writings of the Albigenses have all been destroyed by the Inquisitor, but their confessions of faith, mixed with many falsities, are preserved in the records of their enemies. They were accused of Manicheism or worshipping two gods, one good and one evil; of adoring Lucifer in the form of a black cat; of sorcery and turbulence; of propagating their opinions by fire and sword; of abhorring animal food because it was produced by the evil one; of denying that Christ had a substantial body, and thus doing away with the benefits of his death. All these and many other horrible accusations they denied, and suffered persecution and martyrdom rather than admit that they were true. That they held a Scriptural faith similar to that of the Waldenses and of the Protestant churches to-day is clear. In the year 1017, at Orleans, three priests, converts of the Paulicians, were examined for eight hours, Queen Constance keeping guard at the door of the cathedral, and afterwards with a stick putting out the eye of one of them,—Stephen, who had been her confessor, and who probably had reproved her sins. But "harder than any iron," they refused to repent, were degraded from holy orders, and with other converts, fourteen in all, were led without the walls of the city, where a great fire was kindled, and were burned. These martyrs were said to be Manicheans, who maintained the existence of two gods: an evil god, the creator of the material world, and a good god, the creator of the spiritual world. But they themselves said that they believed in one God, whose law was written in their hearts by the Holy Ghost: "We can see our King reigning in heaven. By His own almighty hand He will raise us up to an immortal tri-

WALDENSIAN CHURCH AT SAN GIOVANNI.

umph, and will speedily bestow upon us joy celestial."

The persistent charge of Manicheism, a pagan religion of the East, was made against the Albigenses because their theological ancestors, the Paulicians or Cathari, were themselves converts from Manicheism in Armenia. About the middle of the seventh century, Constantine, a native of Armenia, from reading the four gospels and the fourteen epistles of St. Paul, abandoned the errors of Manicheism, renounced Manes, accepted the doctrine of the Trinity and of Christ's divinity and incarnation, and led a life of exemplary godliness. He assumed the name of Sylvanus and founded a new Church, the members of which, from admiration of St. Paul, called themselves Paulicians. They protested against the tyranny of Rome, accepted the Bible as the only rule of faith, and purified their creed from all errors of Gnostic theology.

The emperors of the Eastern empire, who were already slaughtering Manicheans, extended their persecutions to these evangelical Christians. Constantine Sylvanus was ordered to be stoned by his own disciples, all of whom but one refused to stone him. Simeon, the imperial officer who directed the persecution, was himself converted, and after struggling with his conscience three years at the Court of Constantinople, returned, became the successor of Sylvanus, and was burned, together with hundreds of the Paulicians, on one huge funeral pile. The few Paulicians who were left continued to proselytize, and the Church increased. But, worn with persecution, they emigrated in the year 755 to the West, passing over Asia into Thrace, then into Bulgaria, then into Italy, and at last into France, where they arrived at the beginning of the eleventh century. This persecuted church of the Paulicians, which was even more cruelly persecuted when it developed in France into the church of the Albigenses, is the other symbolic candlestick. It is the Eastern church, while the Waldensian is the Western. Now, united after unimaginable sorrows, they preach the gospel in Italy, and are a light shining in darkness. *Lux lucet in tenebris.*

# CHAPTER IV

### ANTIQUITY OF THE WALDENSES BEFORE PETER WALDO

ALL Roman Catholic and some Protestant historians call Peter Waldo of Lyons the founder of the ancient Church of the Cottian Alps. This theory sweeps away at a breath not only the Apostolic but the Italian origin of the Waldensian Church, making it no older than the year 1160, when Peter Waldo began his ministry in France. The firm conviction of this people, that they have existed in the Alpine valleys "from time immemorial," is made to yield to the mere fact that Peter, the rich merchant of Lyons, bore the name of Waldo, and left it to his followers in the north of France, in Germany, and in Bohemia. In this latter country he died in 1197, after evangelizing with zeal thirty-seven years.

The Waldenses, except a few recently, have never, during these seven centuries, recognized him as their head. Their oldest writings, their confessions of faith, their catechisms and poems, are not his, and make no mention of him. He could not have founded a Church which by the very confessions of its enemies already existed, and which is well known to have professed in the ninth century evangelical doctrines opposed to those of the Roman Church. He was called Valdo or Valdis, Valdensius, Valdensis, or Valdius, the name appearing in all these slightly varied forms. He received this name from the district where he was born, in Dauphiny in France, the border country, which was also named Valdis or Vaudra, or Valden, from its proximity to the Waldensian valleys of Italy. His family belonged there, and he himself lived there in his youth before becoming a merchant at Lyons. The Protestant inhabitants of Dauphiny were utterly exterminated in later centuries by persecution, their faith being the same as that of the Waldenses on the other side of the Alps.

Nothing but the bias of early education would explain the conduct of Peter Waldo at a great crisis in his life. The sudden death of one of his companions at a banquet made the world and worldly things odious to him. The good seed sown in his childhood and afterwards choked in a thorny soil sprang up to sudden life, and caused him to devote the remainder of his days to the service of Heaven and his fellowmen. Had his early training been in the papal Church, with his riches he would have founded an abbey and entered it as a monk; but he began, instead, to denounce the Roman Church as the Babylon of the Apocalypse, and caused the Scriptures to be translated into the vulgar tongue. He devoted himself altogether to missionary labors, turned his house into a hospital, and distributed his goods to the poor, made proselytes in Lyons, and wandered over many countries teaching a pure Christian doctrine. These were evidently his already adopted sentiments, learned in youth, and neglected during his prosperous worldly life as a merchant.

The sudden religious impression received by Luther under similar circumstances took a different form. Luther was trained a papist from childhood, and when, at twenty years of age, having just finished the course of philosophy at Erfurt, his companion was struck down at his side by lightning during a thunder storm, he abandoned the world by entering a monastery, — not by preaching the gospel, for he did not know it, — not by denouncing the

Roman Church, for he was devoted to it until years after, when, through terrible mental struggles, he was freed from its power. Waldo knew at once, when the spirit touched his heart, what Luther learned only by the might of his intellect, and the throes of his strong heart. Waldo, Le Vaudois, as the French called him, was born to the knowledge of the Scriptures. Imitating the early Christians, he sold all that he had and gave to the poor. "No one," he said, "can serve both God and mammon." Beginning at Pentecost, for three days every week he distributed food to all who came for it. Crowds gathered around him, and his friends exclaimed that he was mad. But, mounting on a convenient place, he said: "Citizens and friends, I am not out of my mind, as you believe, but I am avenging myself on my enemy, — this money, which had reduced me to slavery, and made me more obedient to it than to God; if any one after this shall see me with money, then let him say that I am mad; and may you also learn to place your hope in God, and not in riches." But Peter did not change his condition without pain. The separation from his wife and two daughters, who did not accept his religious ideas, wrung his heart, and he was distressed by the agony of his poor wife, who, having heard that he had asked and obtained alms from an old friend, rushed half wild to the Archbishop, who cited them both to appear before him. She ran to her husband when he came, and between anger and tears cried: "Oh, were it not better that I should do penance for my sins by giving alms to thee rather than to others?" From that day Peter took food only from his wife. The Archbishop of Lyons soon began to persecute Peter and the Poor Men, his disciples, who like him had abandoned their worldly goods. Waldo fled into Picardy, where, three centuries later, John Calvin was born, and then crossed the Alps with some of his followers to find a welcome in Piedmont. Once more he returned to escort other disciples to the same place of shelter. The historian Botta acknowledges that Peter found the Waldenses there. "The Waldenses," he says, "are called thus either because they inhabit the valleys, or because Waldo, a celebrated heretic of the twelfth century, left them his name after having accepted their opinions."

Peter de Bruis and Henry, the Italian, who, half a century before Waldo, had preached in France, where one died in prison and the other at the stake, had prepared the way for his mission. The earnest preaching of the Scriptures, the fervent love and faith showing itself in works of charity of Waldo, soon gained him eighty thousand adherents. He sent men of all ranks, barefooted and without money, into all the surrounding country, ordering them to preach in the public squares, and to penetrate into the houses and churches. They afterwards extended their missionary labors into many other countries of Europe. The persecution in the next century of the Poor Men of Lyons, or Waldenses, and of the Albigenses, who held the same doctrines, filled all the prisons in France. The Roman Catholic bishops of Aix, Arles, and Avignon said that between A.D. 1206 and A.D. 1228, "so great a number of the Waldenses were apprehended that it was not only impossible to nourish them, but to provide lime and stone to build prisons for them." In the year 1212 two religious orders, the Minor Friars or Franciscans, and the Preaching Friars or Dominicans were instituted to combat two sects which "long since sprang up in Italy," says an abbot of the thirteenth century. These two sects, or rather two branches of the same sect, were the "Humiliated" and the

"Perfect," or the Waldenses and the Poor Men of Lyons. Reinerius the Inquisitor calls the latter "modern heretics," to distinguish them from a "much more ancient sect, the Leonists or Waldenses of Piedmont," their theological ancestors.

# CHAPTER V

### THE "NOBLE LESSON"

THE most ancient document of the Waldenses is "La Nobla Leyczon," a poem of four hundred and seventy-nine verses written in an idiom similar to that of the primitive Romaunt languages in Alexandrine verse, without rhyme. "The spirit of this poem," says a Waldensian historian, "is that of a simple and retired age; of a people constantly nourished by pure, primitive doctrine; touching in its simplicity, and beautiful in its tolerance." Its subject is, according to verses 437 and 438, "The three laws that God has given to the world, — the natural law, the law of Moses, and the law of the Gospel." "O brethren, hear a noble lesson. We ought always to watch and pray, for we see that the world is near to its end. We ought to strive to do good works since we see that the world approaches its end. Well have a thousand and a hundred years been entirely completed since it was written that we are in the last times." This remarkable date, contained in the sixth verse of the poem and written thus in the original, —

"Ben ha mil e cent ancz compli entierament,"

fixes the date of its composition at the year 1100 if counted from the Christian era, or at from A.D. 1149 to 1180 if counted from the prophecies of St. Peter and St. John. "Now we are in the last time," says the poet, meaning to give a solemn warning to prepare for the end of the world. It was the general impression of all Christendom that Satan, having been bound through the millennium of one thousand years, was loosed in the year 1000, and that after a short period of persecution of the saints through his minister, Antichrist, the world would be destroyed. The Waldenses believed the Papacy to be the predicted Antichrist, and the Papists saw the loosing of Satan in the great increase of heresy during the eleventh and twelfth centuries. The Waldenses and Albigenses saw a persecuting priesthood whose labors began at Orleans almost immediately after the expiration of the thousand years, and an apostate Church, — the mystic Babylon, — seated on the seven hills of Rome, and they did not hesitate to call it the Man of Sin, or Antichrist. Doubt has been thrown on the antiquity of the Noble Lesson, some historians believing that it was written in the year 1400, three centuries later than the time indicated by its dialect and character.

In the year 1658 Sir Samuel Morland, then English Ambassador at the court of Piedmont, sent four Waldensian manuscripts to the library at Cambridge. One of these was a copy of the Noble Lesson, and in it, between the words *mil* or *thousand* and *cent* or *one* hundred, appears the number IV in Roman characters, making the date A.D. 1400. This copy is of the fifteenth century, and contains besides this error many others. The interpolation of *quatre* or *four* lengthens the verse, a mistake which the same copyist makes in verse 473, while he shortens verse 30. The Noble Lesson has been attributed to Peter Waldo, or to some of his disciples. But, if this were true, why did they not carry with them and leave behind them similar writings in the other countries where they went, or in the south of France, from whence they came? Why was not this ancient poem written in one of the Romaunt dialects of France instead of in an idiom similar to the Italian, and precisely that spoken by the Waldenses? Mr. Raynouard, a student of those languages, says that, judging only from its dialect, the Noble Lesson must be the production of the eleventh or twelfth century. The date 1100, he says, merits all faith, and the style of the work and form of the verses favor its authenticity. Although the poem refers to Roman Catholic intolerance, it says nothing of the Inquisition, and there is a youthful courage and ardor in attacking abuses which yielded afterwards to the accents of pain and grief. The horror which the Noble Lesson expresses of the doctrines of Mariolatry, and saint-worship, of the supremacy of the Pope and the idolatry of the mass, at a period when all the rest of the world blindly obeyed the Papacy, is also a proof that it is the production of mountaineer Waldenses. They all, without distinction, young men and girls and little children, as well as the gray-bearded barbes or ministers, made it a duty to spread the knowledge of the gospel. The Vaudois missionary might assume the garb and carry the lute of the troubadour, singing portions of the "Nobla Leyczon" instead of the Provençal love songs of the period. "They have invented certain verses," says a writer of the thirteenth century, "in which they teach the practice of virtue and the hatred of vice." They taught that "God is the only object of worship; that the Bible is the only rule of faith, and Christ the only foundation of salvation." They believed in one God, — Father, Son, and Holy Spirit; that Christ is Life, Truth, Peace, Righteousness, Shepherd, and Advocate, Sacrifice, and Priest; that He died for the salvation of all believers and rose again for their justification. The troubadours or minstrels went from castle to castle, singing their songs, from the eleventh to the thirteenth centuries, a custom which is mentioned in another Waldensian poem, called "La Barca," known to be a production of the thirteenth century and of later date than the Noble Lesson. All rhymists agree that poems like the Noble Lesson in accented lines are older than those like "La Barca," written in rhyme. Another proof of its antiquity is the peculiar use of the word *baron*, which only at the end of the thirteenth century became a title of nobility. Previous to that time, and especially from the ninth to the eleventh century, it meant only some great or venerable person. In the old Provençal "Song of

Roland" the twelve counsellors of Charlemagne are called "the great barons with white beards," and in the Noble Lesson the three Magi at the cradle of the Saviour are called "the three barons," and Abraham receives the same title. Before the middle of the thirteenth century a titled person would have been called a duke or marquis, and not a baron. Verse 331 of the poem says, "Then sprang up a people newly converted. Christians they were named, for they believed in Christ. But we find here what the Scripture says, that the Jews and Saracens persecuted them grievously." This expression, "Jews and Saracens," applied in general to all persecutors, betrays an epoch when the Saracens were yet objects of terror and the agents of violence against all Christians. They were conquered by Charles Martel in 732, but they continued to ravage France and parts of the French Alps near the Waldensian valleys until the end of the twelfth century. Godfrey of Bouillon took Jerusalem from the Saracens in the year 1099. The Saracen, in the current phraseology of the people of the West, was the typical enemy and persecutor of Christians of their time, as the Jew had been of Christ himself. Another proof of the antiquity of the Noble Lesson is the omission to mention the number of nails used in crucifying the Saviour in the verse: "Four wounds they gave him besides other blows. After that they gave him a fifth to make the completion, for one of the knights came and opened his side, and forthwith there flowed out blood and water mingled together." One of the heresies attributed to the Albigenses and Waldenses was their opinion that three nails only were used, and that the left side of our Lord was pierced by the spear. Triclavianism was condemned by Pope Innocent III., who decided that four nails were used, and that the Roman soldier pierced the right side of Christ.

Saint Francis of Assisi, the founder of one of the two Orders instituted by Innocent III. against the Waldenses, or the "Humiliated," and the Poor Men of Lyons, or the "Perfect," was miraculously marked by the five wounds of the Saviour, so that the four nails were seen, — two on the inside of the hands, and two on the outside of the feet, and the wound on the right side. He contrived to mark himself thus in order to disprove the old triclavian or three-nail heresy of those whom he was appointed to oppose. "The heretics," says a writer of the period, "were confounded by this practical argument of Francis."

Peter Waldo, in 1160, made a translation of the Scriptures into the dialect of Southern France, a proof that he was acquainted with another version of the Bible, probably that of the Italian Waldenses. The Paulicians or Albigenses certainly possessed it, as they were known to have suffered martyrdom for its doctrines in Armenia before emigrating to Europe. The Noble Lesson says: "For the Scripture saith, and we ought to believe it, that all men pass two ways, the good to glory, and the wicked to torment. But if any shall not believe this let him study the Scriptures from the beginning to the end." A reference is made, towards the end of the Waldensian poem, to various celestial phenomena, which occurred during the eleventh century, and were believed to be signs of the approaching end of the world. "Many signs and wonders shall be from this time forward to the day of judgment. May it please the Lord who formed the world that we may be of the number of his elect to stand in his courts. Thanks unto God. Amen."

## CHAPTER VI

### CALUMNIES AND OPPRESSIONS OF THE INQUISITORS

THE Waldenses for many centuries were a persecuted and suffering race. They were accused by their enemies and persecutors of every crime and base practice; of worshipping Lucifer in the form of a black cat; of making a cake of meal with the blood of an infant; of deceiving their proselytes by diabolical means, and inducing them to forsake their holy mother, the Church and the priests, "through whom they ought to come to salvation"; of being sorcerers "who dealt in the impious vanity of magical incantations."

Through all the middle ages the Waldenses of Piedmont were reported to be a race of impious magicians, and the belief in their sorcery was often of use to them in battles with their enemies. It was believed that through special favor of the devil they were proof against musketry, and that their barbes

## Oppressions of the Inquisitors 41

or ministers after a battle gathered up the balls in their skirts by handfuls without having received any harm. The children of these terrific Vaudois were always born, it was said, with hairy throats, with four rows of black teeth, and with a single eye in the middle of their foreheads. One of the Dukes of Savoy, their prince, who visited his Waldensian subjects after a persecution, asked to see these monstrous children, but was convinced of the calumny when rosy, pearly-toothed, well-formed, two-eyed, lovely babies and children were brought to him. The very name of Vaudois or Vaulderie came to mean witchcraft or friendship with the Evil One. "When they wish to go to the said Vaulderie they anoint themselves with an ointment which the devil has given them. They then rub with it also a very small rod of wood, and with the palms of their hands place the rod between their legs. Thus prepared and equipped, they fly away wherever they please, and the devil carries them to the place where they hold their assembly. In that place they find tables ready set out with wine and victuals, and a devil in the shape of a goat with the tail of an ape gives them a meeting."

Yet the Inquisitors who thus excited the

fancy and the hatred of the common people against the Waldenses, in their communications regarding them to each other, were constrained by the divine power of truth to give them another character. As in a mirror, the lovely modesty and humility of the Waldensian character is reflected through the cloud of calumny. "Heretics are the worst and most profligate of mankind," says the Inquisitor. "They are known by their manners and their words. They are composed and modest; they admit no pride of dress, holding a just mean between the expensive and the squalid. In order that they may the better avoid lies, and oaths, and trickery, they dislike entering into trade, but by the labor of their hands they live like ordinary workmen. Their very teachers are mere artisans. Riches they seek not to multiply, but are content with things necessary. In meat and drink they are temperate. They resort neither to taverns, nor to dances, nor to any other vanities. From anger they carefully restrain themselves. They are always engaged either in working, or in learning, or in teaching, and therefore they spend but little time in prayer."

This paradoxical race, so wicked, and yet so practised in all the Christian graces, made converts among the noble and the great. A wandering missionary, with a pack, like any other merchant, would knock at the great doors of a castle, and be admitted to the presence of the beautiful castellana. When he had shown his rings, and robes, and other wares, he would say, "Lady, I have jewels far more precious than these, which I will give you if you will secure me against the priests." The promise given, he said, "I possess a brilliant gem from God himself, for through it man comes to the knowledge of God; and I have another which casts out so ruddy a heat that it forthwith kindles the love of God in the heart of the owner." The "vagabond" then rehearsed parts of the New Testament, and often won the lovely lady of the castle to the "religion," as it was called, even the enemies calling it by that name, as if there were no other religion. St. Bernard, the enemy of the Albigenses, described them thus: "If you ask them of their faith, nothing can be more Christian, nothing more irreprehensible than their conversation, and what they say they confirm by their deeds. They attack no one; they circumvent no one; they defraud no one. Their faces are pale with fasting; they eat not the bread of idleness." Yet, "mark the fox," says Bernard, as he proceeds to enumerate some of the popular calumnies, forgetting that this good fruit could scarcely grow upon an evil tree. "They submitted joyfully and triumphantly to martyrdom, rather than apostatize from what they held to be the true faith of the gospel."

But this contempt of death and suffering was, in heretics, "inspired by Satan, and the martyrdom was spurious." If by torture or fear of worldly loss they were tempted to retract and abjure their faith, as soon as "ever they became masters of their own actions they forthwith returned to wallowing in the filth of their pristine error." These contradictory accounts given of the Vaudois and of their brothers, the Albigenses, by their enemies, are noted also in the Nobla Leyczon, verses 357 and 372. "If any one will not curse, nor swear, nor lie, nor commit injustice or larceny, nor be dissolute, nor avenge himself on his enemies, they say he is a Vaudois, and merits to be punished." "These heretics," confessed King Louis XII., in speaking of his Vaudois subjects of Val Louise, "are better Christians than we." The Waldenses of Piedmont were always distinguished, says Léger, one of their own historians, by "a simple and sincere conformity to the sacred Word, by a holy life and conversation, by persecution and the cross." Culture of the fields and care of the flocks have always been the principal occupations of the inhabitants of the Cottian Alps. They are intelligent, but the centuries of oppression which had weighed upon them until a recent period made them apathetic and concentrated in themselves. Their type is far from being vulgar. They are tall, or at least of more than medium height; their black hair is fine and slightly curly; their forehead is high and broad; the eyebrows are heavy; the nose is fine, the chin well-shaped. They are sober, patient, laborious; slow to accept innovations, but faithful to their promises. "Those who know the idiom of the Waldenses as it is spoken in these mountains," says Muston, one of their historians, "can read the old poems that are attributed to the race." A French historian, M. Henri Martin, says: "It cannot be doubted that there has been in the high Alps of Piedmont and Dauphiny a population which has preserved, from ancient times, traditions and manners very different from those which have prevailed in the Roman Church." These may be only tendencies, but in a rural and retired population they are the result of hereditary traditions and habits handed down from generation to generation. It might be supposed that such a life of hardship and toil, such centuries of sorrow and persecution would sink the Waldensian to the level of his herd; but, on the contrary, he is gentle and courteous in manner. On the highest mountain, or in the loneliest vale, the traveller among them is sure of safety and welcome. He speaks with a tone of melancholy, as if the sorrows of his ancestors had branded themselves on his soul. Until the year 1848, when Charles Albert, King of Sardinia, gave a charter of liberty to them and to Italy, they had still their sorrows and privations. They were forbidden to occupy or to purchase land beyond certain boundaries, and a minister could not visit a sick person beyond those limits unless accompanied by a Romish layman, and even then could not stay more than twenty-four hours. All correspondence with foreign ministers was prohibited, and heavy duties were imposed on all books, and especially on Bibles and religious works. Their physicians, surgeons, apothecaries, lawyers, or notaries could not exercise their professions beyond the limits of the valleys. They were forbidden to inclose

## Oppressions of the Inquisitors 47

their burial-grounds with walls. If the child of a Waldensian was stolen, for the purpose of proselytizing, by a Papist, the Waldensian had no redress, even if the Papist on the street called him a heretic and a dog. They were compelled to abstain from work on Popish festivals, and to uncover the head to any idol carried along the streets. This was nearly two centuries after the persecutions of blood in Piedmont had ceased. These were the tender mercies of that power which had persecuted and calumniated their forefathers. "It was a wind of death from the Vatican which caused so many heads to fall; which destroyed so many families; which desolated so many hearts. Terrible hill," says Muston, "which has preserved of Olympus only the false gods, of Sinai only the thunders, and of Calvary only the blood."

# CHAPTER VII

## GEOGRAPHICAL POSITION AND COLONIES

Where are these valleys which "the Eternal God destined as the theatre of his wonders and the asylum of his ark?" These Alpine mountains were the scenes of heroism and suffering, of cruelty and outrage that made the name ring through the world. The rocky but beloved land of the heroic men of the valleys is on the Italian side of the giant wall that separates Italy from France. It lies about thirty miles southwest of Turin, across the broad, level sea of verdure called the Plain of Piedmont, and is a part of the chain of mountains that rises abruptly from the plain.

From Turin, on a clear day, these mountains seem like etherial regions let down to earth, vaporous against the blue sky, the white of the snowy glaciers mingling with the fleecy white clouds. The Waldensian valleys lie between Mount Cenis and Mount Viso, with the French province of Dauphiny

## Geographical Position and Colonies 49

on the west, and the Plain of Piedmont on the east. Persecution and confiscation have reduced them to a space twenty-two miles long and sixteen wide, an area of not over three hundred square miles, the tour of which could be made on foot in twenty hours. Mount Viso, 12,000 feet high, with its snow-crested cone, is like a pyramid rising out of a sea of mountain ridges. It is "the Jungfrau of the South; the powerful spirit that watches over the valleys, for in the shade of its granite sides the torch of the gospel found refuge for its light." The valleys are three: the valley of Luserna or Val-Pellice, including those of Angrogna and Rora; the valley of Perosa and the valley of San Martino. Luserna is watered by the river Pellice, and San Martino by the river Germanasca, — torrents rather than rivers and not navigable, but fretting their way through narrow defiles or spreading out where the green valley permits it to a wider stream. Luserna is the largest and most delightful of these valleys, and its long, low hills, covered with vines and mulberries, border a kind of gulf of the green Plain of Piedmont, which enters there. From this entrance of the valleys there is a lovely view of the plain with the towns scattered over it, and of the rock of Cavour, a mountain rising solitary like a natural fortress. In Luserna grow all kinds of grain, grapes, chestnuts, figs, and delicious fruits. It is a soft, Italian climate: a land of brilliant-hued skies, of bright fire-flies, of trailing vines and fragrant flowers. But the aspect of the country changes farther on in the valleys, and gives place to the wild grandeur of the mountains. Perosa is less fertile than Luserna, and the cold winds of winter, the snow and ice, are sooner felt. The rich vegetation and depths of green, broken by sunlight, give place to forests of chestnuts and walnuts that shade the ground below, and form a thick canopy overhead. San Martino is entirely shut in by the mountains, — a long and narrow valley separated from Luserna by an enormous chain of mountains. The summits of these mountains form a plain, very uneven and completely bare, where, in the depressions of the rocks, accumulate the waters of the rains and melted snows in innumerable pools, some of which are so large as to merit the title of lakes, and to give the region the name of the Plain of the Thirteen Lakes. At the extremities of this mountain plain are two peaks, — the Chalance and the Cournaout, 8,229 and 8,604 feet high.

In the valley of San Martino the eagle builds her nest on the high rocks, and the chamois beguiles the hunter to the chase. High mountain peaks, crowned with eternal snows, rise on every side, and the lower slopes of the hills are dotted with pretty towns and farmhouses surrounded by orchards and vineyards. Here grow many lovely Alpine flowers, one of which, the blue Campanula Elatinus, is celebrated for its delicate beauty.

The river of San Martino, the Germanasca, that spreads out broad and calm above, is narrowed at its outlet to a few yards in width, and struggles through the rocky defile with noise and foam. This is a peculiarity of these mountain rivers: the Rospart, that issues at Villar, in the valley of Perosa, is so covered with verdure that it can be seen only when near, and the Subiasc, a tributary of Pellice, issues at Bobi from a gorge so narrow that it is only visible exactly in front. Luserna has ten beautiful towns, and La Tour, the capital, is so named from the tower which was anciently the castle on the hill behind the town. Every name brings up a throng of memories, — Angrogna, Villar, Bobi, Rora, — where every rock has been wet with blood, and every meadow has seen the death of martyrs. Perosa has six towns and San Martino eleven. These are the actual Waldensian Valleys, but there were others on the French side of the Alps, once inhabited by the Waldensians, from which they were banished. Val Louise, in Dauphiny, was once full of "heretics," but none are there now, and the inhabitants are even ignorant of the bloody history of their ancestors.

In Val Clusone, or Val de Pragela, which is connected with San Martino by a narrow pass, the Col du Pis, they were exterminated by persecution, exile, and confiscation of their goods. Val Cluson or Pragela in France joined Val Perosa in Piedmont, and, as the inhabitants were all brothers of one faith, one of the towns, La Chapelle, was half in France, and half in Italy, — the church on one side of the line, and the house of the pastor on the other. The Waldensians have disappeared also from the valleys of Queyras, Mathias, and Meane, where they once existed. These French valleys, which were already peopled by evangelical Christians became the refuge of the disciples of Waldo in the twelfth century. The Italian Waldenses, in the year 1495, sent a colony of farmers into Provence, which flourished and so increased in number

## Geographical Position and Colonies 53

and influence that the attention of the Inquisitors was attracted to it, and it was exterminated by fire and sword. They sent a colony in the fourteenth century to Calabria and the Puglie in southern Italy, which increased in wealth and founded several towns. These were all destroyed, and their inhabitants murdered, driven away or forced to apostatize, while their pastor, John Louis Pascal, was burned at Rome. They had a colony which was exterminated at Saluzzo, in Piedmont; another at Cuneo, and another at Busca. "The Evangelicals," says an Inquisitor, "were not only numerous in the valleys, where they were called Mountaineers or Vallenses, but, not satisfied with being hidden in the caves of the mountains, they had the audacity to sow their false doctrines in the plains of Piedmont and of Lombardy, and to establish themselves at Bagnolo, so that they were called Bagnolese." At Mantua, at Brescia, at Bergamo, at Vicenza, at Florence, at Spoleto, they were known under various names.

A manuscript, believed to be of the twelfth century, says that their missions were even further extended. "Merchants of that people in the Alps who learn the Bible by heart and combat the rites of the Church, which they say are new, reach Switzerland, Bavaria and upper Italy." They had houses in Florence, Genoa, and Venice, the latter city alone containing six thousand Waldenses. Long before the Reformation they existed in Italy, France, and Germany. Their open friendship with the German Reformers and the renewed zeal of their own Christian life kindled such fires of persecution that their numbers diminished. In the year 1622 the College of the Propaganda Fede was established in Rome to persecute them. In 1686 the entire population of the Piedmontese Waldensian valleys was put to death or sent into exile, and Italy at last was freed from the "heretic." But in three years and a half they returned. Nine hundred warriors, an heroic band, crossed Lake Leman at night; in ten days climbed the dreadful mountains of Savoy, and took possession of their homes in San Martino, Perosa, and Luserna. Since then they have suffered no bloody persecution, and now all Italy is theirs to evangelize according to their means and ability. But alas! it is still — *Lux lucet in tenebris!*

# CHAPTER VIII

### THE MINISTERS, OR "BARBES"

THE pastors of the Waldenses were by them familiarly called "barbes," a Piedmontese word, meaning "uncle," used in perilous times in order to conceal their office. The Papists called all who recognized the barbes for pastors, barbets. The barbes were acknowledged, even by some of their adversaries, to be lovers of virtue and enemies of vice. The papal clergy in the passion of persecution often accused them of mysterious crimes, but these calumnies were always disproved by investigations made before the magistrates of the places the Waldenses inhabited. The monks could never show proof of the truth of these stories which were only invented to respond to the revelations made by the pastors of the corruptions in the Church of Rome. A monk, for instance, would say that in his youth he had heard things which he would not repeat and much less write; and that he knew well some of the barbes appeared honest and religious, but he had heard said that there were others of their religion who were not so. He dared not name persons, places, or any particular facts, but contented himself with saying that "there were persons yet living who remembered that their fathers did so and so." When pressed to be more explicit, he would say that he meant not to defame the Waldenses; but these were things he had seen written in a book, the author of which he had forgotten or would not name. But many bishops, priests, monks, and historians of the Roman Catholic Church have testified to the honesty and good conduct of the barbes, and also to their piety towards God and their charity to men, admitting that their only fault was denying the authority of "Holy Mother Church," and not acknowledging it as the true Church nor its superstitions as means of salvation.

Pierre Gilles, the historian of the Waldenses in the sixteenth century, says that "so many books written by the pastors in various places and during many centuries testify in what esteem they held virtue and good works and what hatred they felt for every form of vice." Unfortunately many of these books were lost

CASCADE OF THE PIS AT MASSELLO.

SCHOOL OF THE BARBES AT PRÀ DEL TORNO, ANGROGNA.

## The Ministers, or "Barbes"

during the persecutions of the seventeenth century and only those books and ancient documents sent to the libraries of Cambridge and Geneva by Pastor Léger were preserved. The Papists took care after every persecution to destroy as much of the Waldensian literature as possible. Many of the barbes were learned men and well versed in the languages and science of the Scriptures. A knowledge of the Bible was the distinctive feature of the ancient and is now of the modern Vaudois, and it was so especially of the barbes, all of whom could repeat the Gospels of Saint Matthew and Saint John, and a part of the Epistles from memory.

Deprived for centuries of a visible church, and forced to worship in caves and dens, this intimate knowledge of God's Word was their only light. Their school was in the almost inaccessible solitude of a deep mountain gorge called Pra del Tor, and their studies were severe and long-continued, embracing the Latin, Romaunt, and Italian languages. After several years of study and retirement, they were consecrated by the laying-on of hands and receiving the communion. They were supported by the voluntary subscriptions of the people, a division of the collections being made once a year at the general synod; one-third to the ministers, one-third to the poor, and one-third to the missionaries. But they were not entirely dependent on these contributions, as every barbe learned some manual trade or a profession. The greater number were physicians or surgeons, but many were artisans, and all knew how to cultivate the fields and care for the flocks and herds. Before the invention of printing they copied large portions of the Scriptures for the use of their scholars, to whom they also taught the languages and instructed them in piety and good works. They visited the sick, whether called or not; selected arbiters in disputes; admonished those who conducted themselves ill, and sometimes excommunicated the incorrigible.

The ancient barbes of the valleys spoke and used in their writings a language which was a mixture of the Waldensian idiom and of that of the surrounding countries. But the pastors sent from Geneva after the pest in the sixteenth century, which deprived the Waldenses of nearly all their barbes, introduced the French language into the valleys. The missionaries always spoke the languages of the people they visited, this being the

## The Ministers, or "Barbes" 59

object of their diligent study of languages in youth at the college of Pra del Tor. Every year in September the barbes held a general Council or Synod to review the work of each one; to examine and ordain young ministers and to select the missionaries who were to visit the distant churches in Italy and other countries.

These missions generally lasted two years, and the barbes went two by two; an old man called the *Regidor*, and a young one called the *Coadjuteur*. In almost every city of Italy they had numerous secret adherents who welcomed them with joy. Even in papal Rome there were many who looked for their coming and gave them hospitality. How beautiful from the mountains seemed the feet of these bearers of glad tidings to the dwellers in the spiritual desert, and the short and blessed season of their stay gave rich fruits to the Alpine Church. Every pastor was a missionary in his turn; the younger ones being thus initiated in the delicate labor of evangelization under the care of a disciplined veteran, his superior, to whom he was bound to render obedience and deference. The older missionary thus prepared successors worthy of himself and of the Church, and at last, when age no longer permitted these fatiguing journeys, reposed in some parish of the valleys from which he was not moved until death. The great success which attended these missions in the south of Italy in the thirteenth, fourteenth, and fifteenth centuries was proved by the bitter cry of the Roman Church against the spread of gospel truth and by the persecutions which followed. The missionary zeal of the Waldenses was one of the chief causes of the persecutions which they endured. "These Waldenses," said Bernard de Foucald in the twelfth century, "although condemned by Pope Lucius II., continued to pour forth with daring effrontery, far and wide, all over the world, the poison of their perfidy."

The barbes accepted with joy the missionary charge given to them by the synod, although they knew well all the dangers and fatigues of these journeys. A Vaudois preacher, going one day into a church at Florence, where there were several thousand people, heard his mission denounced from the pulpit by a monk in these words: "O Fiorenza, what does thy name mean? The flower of Italy. And that thou wast until these Ultramontanes persuaded thee that man is justified by faith and not by works, and herein they lie." The

## The Ministers, or "Barbes"

pastors came to the synods from all parts of Europe to preserve union among themselves and maintain the uniformity of their church service. At one of these synods, in Val Cluson, there were one hundred and forty pastors, and at the synod of Champforans, after the German Reformation, many of the German ministers came to confer with them. The barbes were generally unmarried, in order to be free for their long journeys, from which they often never returned. They had no religious scruples against matrimony, but would not leave behind them weeping wives and fatherless children, when often their days must end in the prisons of the Inquisition or at the stake. The noblest martyrs were barbes who met death by fire or torture joyfully or patiently in the horrible dungeons of the Inquisition. John Louis Pascal was strangled and burned, and his ashes thrown into the Tiber, at Rome, in the year 1560; Geoffroy Varaglia was burned in the public square of the castle at Turin; another minister, with white beard and lovely countenance, so charmed the executioners that none would put him to death, although they were ordered to do so, and he escaped unharmed to the valleys.

Cesar Baronius, a cardinal, and the librarian

of the Vatican in the sixteenth century, when in Piedmont, knew some of the Vaudois pastors, and often lamented to them the corruption of the Roman Church, especially in the profanation of the Holy Sacrament. "Weep and lament," he said, "for the profanation of this divine mystery. O God! the zeal of thine house hath eaten me up. Impiety, idolatry, ambition, and venality surround thine altars."

Yet he dared not openly abandon Rome, which forgave his invectives on account of his submission to her will. The Vaudois pastors were less eloquent, but more courageous, yielding their bodies to the rack and the flames, but keeping their faith. "Our rule of conduct," said they, "should be the word of Jesus: 'He who will confess me on the earth I will confess in Heaven, and I will deny him in Heaven who has denied me on earth.' We prefer to be repulsed by the Papacy rather than by our Saviour."

WALDENSIAN CHURCH AT ANGROGNA.

# CHAPTER IX

### PERSECUTION BEGUN IN THE YEAR 1476

THE Waldenses have some tradition, or record, of thirty-three persecutions, by which their colonies in Calabria, Apuglie, Provence, the Plain of Piedmont, and in the Alps of France were utterly exterminated. Continual exile, martyrdom, and confiscations of their goods for many centuries also reduced their numbers and their strength in the valleys of Piedmont. In the year 1308 a synod of five hundred delegates was held in the valley of Angrogna. The Inquisitors, with their assistants, then invaded the valley, but were repulsed, and the Roman Catholic prior was killed in the skirmish. Little is known of this and of other persecutions before the year 1476, when Yolande, surnamed Violante from the violence of her character, the widow of Amedeus IX., Duke of Savoy, ordered the Waldenses to return immediately to the Roman Church. For no other reason than their belief, she commanded her nobles to reduce these hardy mountaineers to silence. An investigation made by the Holy See showed the profound difference between the religion of the Waldenses and of the Roman Church, and Pope Innocent VIII. issued a bull of extermination, ordering all nations to arm and destroy them. He absolved from all sins and from any vows they had made those who should put heretics to death. He also annulled all contracts made in favor of Waldenses; ordered their servants to abandon them; forbade any one to give them aid, and authorized robbing them of their possessions.

Thousands of volunteers, vagabonds, fanatics, adventurers, assassins, and robbers gathered from all parts of Italy to execute the commands of the pretended successor of Saint Peter. This horde of brigands, in 1488, marched to the valleys, together with eighteen thousand regular troops, furnished by Charles I. of Piedmont, the son of Yolande or Violante, and by the King of France. The persecuted people were accused of no crime, even in the pontiff's bull of extermination, except the "seducing of their neighbors by an appearance of extreme sanctity." But God, in whom they trusted, raised his arm for their

## Persecution begun in 1476

defence. The Israel of the Alps were inspired by superhuman courage, while the hearts of their persecutors seemed filled with unnatural fear.

The legate of the Pope, Archdeacon Albert Cattanée, before beginning this cruel work, established himself in a convent at Pinerolo, a town at the entrance of the valleys, and sent forward preaching monks to convert the Waldenses by their arguments. These missionaries had no success, and the army then advanced into the valleys. The Waldenses made a touching appeal to the hard heart of their persecutor. "Do not condemn us without a hearing, for we are Christians, and faithful subjects. Our barbes are ready to prove that our doctrines are those of the Word of God. We acknowledge no other authority than the Bible, and are happy in a pure and simple life. We despise the love of riches and the thirst for domination by which our persecutors are devoured. Our trust in God is greater than our desire to please men. Have a care not to call down His wrath upon yourselves in persecuting us, and know that if God so wills all the force that you have gathered against us can do nothing."

And so it was: for the long lines of

Cattanée's army, spread out weakly over the plains, were broken everywhere, and the battalions that came to crush the hydra of heresy were driven back in precipitous flight. The inhabitants had withdrawn to the mountain heights, from whence they could easily descend to attack the enemy in the plains, using swords, arrows, and pickaxes for weapons, and protecting themselves by great shields hastily made of the bark of chestnut trees, lined with skins of animals. Full of address and vigor, and, above all, full of confidence in God, and well placed for defence, they killed many of the foe, and had but little loss themselves. But they were nearly overcome on the heights of San Giovanni or Saint John, leading to the mountains of Angrogna, a natural fortress, where they had taken their families for refuge. Seeing the enemy mounting step by step, and drawing their ranks closer, the women, children, and old men fell on their knees, crying out all together, with fervor born of great distress, "O our God, help us! O God, give ours strength! O God, save us."

"My men shall give you the answer," cried one of the chiefs of the invaders, surnamed Noir de Mondovi on account of his dark complexion, scorning their prayers. But raising

FROM ANGROGNA TO PRÀ DEL TORNO.

his visor at that moment, to prove how little fear he had of these poor people, this new Goliath was struck between the eyes and killed by a stone from the hand of Pierre Revel of Angrogna. The Waldenses, seizing the moment of panic and terror which took possession of the invading troops, made an impetuous attack, and drove them down the mountain vanquished and dispersed to the plain. Then on the mountain, with their delivered families, they threw themselves upon their knees to render thanks to the God of armies, who had given them this signal victory. Even their enemies were soon persuaded that God fought with the heroic mountaineers. When Cattanée the next day organized a new expedition by another road up the valley of Angrogna, hoping to reach the height of Pra del Tor, from which he would have been master of all the country near, a fog — one of those which suddenly arise in the Alps — fell upon them just as they entered the most difficult and dangerous paths.

Unacquainted with the roads, and marching single file over these rocks, on the edge of precipices, they yielded at the first attack of the Waldenses, and were easily defeated. Those in front fell back hastily upon the others; disorder followed; the retreat became a flight, and the flight a catastrophe. Many fell over the slippery precipices which the fog hid from view; some were lost in the ravines, and a few only succeeded in escaping. This decisive victory, due more to the will of God than to the valor of the Waldenses, caused the deliverance of the valley, as Cattanée did not return.

To this day, after four centuries, the place where the captain of this ill-fated expedition, Saguet de Planghère, fell over the rocks, is called by his name. Not only in Angrogna, but on all the mountains near, where they were attacked, the Waldenses defended themselves with heroic courage. Favored by the nature of the places, they put the crusaders to flight by rolling down upon them avalanches of rocks, and then descending to fight hand to hand. The Legate of the Pope transferred his operations to Dauphiny in the Val Louise, where he pillaged and persecuted the unfortunate inhabitants. Seven hundred of his troops, returning drunk with the massacres they had committed in Dauphiny, entered in disorder a village of the Valley of San Martino, believing themselves conquerors there also. But, suddenly attacked on every side, they were all killed or put to flight, the standard-bearer alone escaping to a ravine, where he remained two days, and then crept forth frozen and famished to beg charity of the Vaudois.

This was granted with the generous forgetfulness of injury which Christ inspires in his faithful servants, and he was sent home to report the total defeat of his companions. This army, which seemed so formidable, faded away like clouds before the sun. It was said to this martyr people, "Fear not, little flock, for it is your Father's good pleasure to give you the kingdom; and if God be for you who can be against you?"

The Duke of Savoy withdrew his own troops; sent away the legate on pretence that his mission was terminated, and himself met representatives of the different Vaudois churches at Pinerolo, to discuss the terms of peace. It was during these conferences that the Prince asked to see some of those children who, he believed, were born with black teeth and horned feet. "Is it possible," he said, when they were brought to him, "that these charming creatures are the children of heretics? They are the most beautiful children I have ever seen."

# CHAPTER X

### PERSECUTION OF A.D. 1561

NEVER was the promise of God, "Call upon Me in the day of trouble and I will deliver thee," more clearly fulfilled than it was to the martyr Waldenses in the general persecution of the year 1561. The invasion which threatened to annihilate them was converted into the most brilliant campaign which these heroes had ever made, and they compelled their enemies to retire from the valleys. Nearly a century had passed since the last general persecution of the valleys of Piedmont,— years marked by the most bloody persecutions of their brethren in Provence, and by continual vexations and martyrdoms of themselves.

The German Reformation had revived their faith, and at the Synod of Champforans, in Angrogna, when Farel and other Reformers met with them, they vowed to confess their opinions more courageously than before.

The clouds grew darker and darker over the valleys from that time.

Their friends in Switzerland, in Germany, and in Dauphiny exhorted them to put their trust in God, and deputies from Pragela, in Dauphiny, met with those of Luserna, to renew the alliance between these churches of the Alps. On one of the snowy Alpine heights they swore eternal friendship in the name of their God. It was a scene worthy of the ancient ages, — more romance than history.

The day after, Jan. 21, 1561, a decree was published in the valleys, ordering all the Waldenses to attend mass. If their decision was not made within twenty-four hours they were subject to all the punishments reserved for heretics, — the galleys, the cord, the stake, and the gallows. In this sad extremity the Waldenses offered ardent prayers to God for deliverance, counsel, and guidance, and with one voice decided that as they would not abjure, and it was impossible for them to find a refuge elsewhere, they would defend their lives and their homes unto the death. "Even the smallest worm," says the naïve ancient chronicler, "will do that."

The barbes of Luserna and of Pragela,

standing in the midst of a dense crowd of believers, promised, in their name, with their hands upon the Bible, to keep that sacred Word of God entire according to the usage of the ancient Apostolic Church, and to persevere in their holy religion even at the peril of their lives in order to transmit it whole and pure to their children. "We promise aid and succor to our persecuted brethren, without regard to our individual interests, but to the common cause, not regarding man, but God." Scarcely was this solemn vow taken than several voices cried out with enthusiasm:— "A shameful abjuration is asked of us to-morrow; let us to-morrow make a strong protest against the persecuting idolatry which demands it of us." Patience and humility were exhausted, and the time to show energy had come. Before dawn the next morning, instead of going to the mass, they crowded, armed, to the Protestant temple of Bobi, and cleared it of the rosaries, the candles, and the images with which the Romanists had filled it; their minister preaching afterwards, from Isaiah xlv. 20, — "They have no knowledge that set up the wood of their graven image, and pray unto a god that cannot save."

Encouraged by the eloquence of their minister, the people set out for Villar, three miles distant, singing inspiring hymns as they went, to purge the temple there also of idols. This was a childish iconoclastic act of destruction, but the first step in the drama that was to follow, as every man knew that by this act his life and goods were forfeited.

The twenty-four hours of grace were ended, and the Waldenses of Bobi met the garrison of Villar, which had gone out to make them prisoners. They drove them back to the town, and besieged the fortress, where the monks, the judges, the lords, and gentlemen took refuge. They placed sentinels, and prepared ammunition, and the next day drove back the troops from Torre Pellice, which came to relieve the besieged. Three times during the next ten days they drove back the rescuing troops, until the besieged, reduced to extremities for want of water and provisions, and ignorant of the attempts at rescue made by their friends, gave themselves up on condition that their lives should be saved, and that they should be accompanied to their own camp by two pastors. "They showed thus," says quaint Peter Gilles, "how much they trusted these hated ministers."

This victory caused the traitorous leader of the invading army, the Count of Trinity, to devise a new method of warfare. As he could not vanquish them united in their native mountains, he resolved to disunite them by fair means or foul, before destroying them. He sent a gentle message to the inhabitants of the Valley of Angrogna, that they had nothing to fear from him, provided they refrained from mixing with the affairs of the other valleys. But, taught by bitter experience, the Waldenses were not deceived, and returned no answer. They made intrenchments, established posts and signals, prepared ammunition, and organized bands of "flying companies," with bows and arrows. These youthful heroes were always accompanied in their sallies by two pastors, who calmed their excesses of anger and prevented useless effusion of blood.

The righteousness of their cause must be proved by the justice of their conduct, and every morning and evening, as well as at the beginning and end of every battle they knelt to ask for grace and guidance in this hard extremity. A second attack was easily repulsed, and the third became a terrible rout for the invaders, and a glorious victory for

ANGROGNA.

the Waldenses. The Count of Trinity, who had brought all his forces and employed all his strategy to vanquish the despised enemy, wished to surprise Pra del Tor, the citadel on the heights of Angrogna, a green oasis shut in by terrible rocks and precipices. There the persecuted people had retired, carrying with them mills and furnaces, and all things necessary for subsistence. The invader divided his army into three parts, to approach the strong place from different points; but this division proved his ruin, for one by one the parts of his army were vanquished and almost destroyed. They fled before the victorious "flying companies," and, unable to mount as rapidly as the others came down, were driven over precipices and into ravines. Two of their chiefs were killed, and one of them was beheaded with his own sword. They would have been exterminated without the intervention of the pastors, who ran to the place of carnage to defend those who could no longer defend themselves. "To death! to death!" cried the young Vaudois, excited by the ardor of their victory. "No! on your knees," cried the pastor, "to thank the God of battles for the success that He has given us."

All that day in green Pra del Tor the

families of these warriors had prayed without ceasing, and when at evening they knew that the prayer had been answered, they made the rocks echo with songs of joy and triumph, and praises to God. The victors returned with arms and booty taken from their enemies, and never had the wild rocks of Pra del Tor witnessed such a collection of swords, poignards, halberds, and cuirasses.

In revenge for this defeat, the Count of Trinity burned the town of Rora, not far from Villar, and drove the people to the snowy heights of a mountain near, where the night surprised them. But they saw the bonfires, and heard the songs of joy at Villar, and took courage to press on to their friends.

Many other efforts were made by the persecuting army to subdue the Waldenses, but without success. "To-day we shall sweep these heretics away," said one of these soldiers, as they started for the attack. "Sir," said his hostess, "if our religion is better than theirs you will have the victory, if not, it is you who will be swept away." The fear of them fell on all the invaders, and the soldiers at last refused to join the army of the Count of Trinity. Hundreds fell in every attack, while the Waldenses lost only fourteen in all these battles. It was said that the death of one Waldensian cost that of one hundred of their enemies. The latter were half vanquished at the mere idea of meeting these invincible foes, and a panic of terror took hold of them before a battle began, for they said, "Certainly God is with them, and we do wrong." The Count of Trinity himself sat on a rock one day after a defeat, weeping for the death of a friend killed in the attack. He made another treacherous assault in the midst of a truce proposed by himself, but was repulsed, as usual, with great loss, and, falling sick, his army was recalled. The Duke of Savoy, Emanuel Philibert, then at Cavour, granted to his ever-faithful subjects amnesty for the past, liberty of conscience, return of the banished, and permission for apostates to return to their faith. This clemency was due to the influence of a woman — Margaret, Duchess of Savoy — who was a Protestant.

# CHAPTER XI

### PERSECUTION OF EASTER, 1655

"To propagate the faith and to extirpate heretics," was the motto of the Congregation of the Propaganda, founded in Rome in the year 1622. The Council of Trent before that had recommended the persecution of "depraved heretics," and the Council of Constance had declared that no faith was to be kept with them. The most conspicuous persecutor of the Waldenses in the seventeenth century, the Marquis of Pianezza, in Turin, found, therefore, authority in his Church for all the cruelty and perfidy which he practised on the defenceless Israel of the Alps.

Jesuitism had destroyed in him the honor of a soldier, and all nobility of character. He was perfidious, but courteous; cruel but devout, and he hesitated to employ no means that would serve his end. He was guilty, in Passion Week of the year 1655, of an act of perfidy without precedent, even in the history of the Waldenses. The Council of "propaganda fide et extirpandis hæreticis," of Turin, of which Pianezza was a member, was composed of the highest dignitaries of the court of the Duke of Savoy, Charles Emanuel II. It met regularly at the residence of the Archbishop, and had subordinate councils established in all parts of Piedmont to spy out and persecute the Waldenses.

It urged the Duke of Savoy to cruelties and oppressions foreign to his character, which placed him in a shameful position before the other nations of Europe.

"The spirit of the Papacy alone," says Muston, "aroused this tempest. Rome was the cause of all! Rome, barbarous and persecuting!"

The decree of January, 1655, ordered all the heads of families in nine villages of the lower valleys to retire within three days to Bobi, Villar, Angrogna, and Rora, the only places where "the religion" would be tolerated, and to sell, during the twenty days following, all their houses and lands unless they consented to become Roman Catholics. They obeyed, but sent deputies to Turin to represent their distress to the Duke, who referred them to the Council. The Council refused to receive them because they were Protestants, and obliged them to select a Roman Catholic to plead their cause, who was forced to present their petition for clemency upon his knees. Three months were consumed in this way, delegation after delegation being sent by the men of the valleys to treat with their foes without obtaining relief or redress. While the last of these delegations was at Turin, waiting the pleasure of Pianezza to receive them, he had treacherously left the city with his army, and was already at the entrance of the valleys. On the eve of Palm Sunday he appeared before Torre Pellice and the few inhabitants remaining there, ordering them to lodge eight hundred of his men and three hundred horses.

All that moonlight night the Waldenses resisted his entrance to their town, and when assailed in the rear by a part of Pianezza's troops, led by one who knew the roads through the fields and gardens, they fled through the ranks of their enemies to the heights.

Thus began that Holy Week of 1655, which the Papists celebrated by a horrible massacre and incredible acts of perfidy.

During the night the invaders sang the "Te Deum," and in the morning, after mass,

## Persecution of Easter, 1655

sallied forth to the villages and farmhouses, to chase the heretics, killing all they found by the way, and burning houses after destroying the inmates.

That night new troops arrived, making the invading army fifteen thousand men.

It was no longer possible to doubt that the old project of the extermination of the Waldenses, so long fomented and acknowledged by the most zealous in the Roman Church, was at last to be executed. The poor mountaineers, ill prepared for defence, and in numbers one to a hundred of the enemy, were attacked at Torre Pellice, St. John, Angrogna, and Bricherasio, but drove back the invaders on Monday and Tuesday, losing two men and killing fifty.

Pianezza then employed perfidy, a weapon which has often succeeded in vanquishing the Waldenses.

On Wednesday morning, two hours before daybreak, he sent trumpeters and messengers, inviting them to confer with him and establish peace with his Royal Highness, the Duke of Savoy. He gave the deputies from all the towns an excellent dinner, and persuaded them that the inhabitants of the higher valleys had nothing to fear. He professed to be pained at the excesses that had been committed by his soldiers, and spoke of the difficulty of restraining so large a number of men, expressing a strong desire to send most of them back to Turin. If each town would receive and lodge a few of them, thus giving the Duke a proof of their loyalty and confidence, he could send back the remainder, and the towns of the lower valleys would be treated with less rigor.

Deceived by these fair promises, the deputies agreed to receive the soldiers of the Marquis of Pianezza, and that same evening permitted them to enter their houses and take possession of their strong places. The murderers, impatient to begin the massacre which had been secretly ordered, killed some of the people that night, and set fire to a village called Taillaret. The blaze of the burning houses, the cries of the fugitives, and the shouts of the persecutors convinced the inhabitants of the valleys too late of their fatal mistake. They lighted bonfires on the heights as signals of distress, and sent messengers from village to village to warn the people against the traitors. But they were now in the power of the enemy, and at four o'clock, on Saturday morning, the day before Easter,

## Persecution of Easter, 1655

the signal for the general massacre so long in preparation was given.

Rested and refreshed, the murderers turned to kill their hosts, who had kindly received them. The horrors which followed are beyond description. A cry of anguish rose from every house. Little children were torn from the arms of their mothers and beaten against the rocks, and the old and the sick — women as well as men — burned in their beds, or hacked in pieces, or mutilated, or skinned, or left dying in the sun, and exposed to wild beasts. Others were tied naked, like a ball, with the head between the legs, and rolled over the precipices.

A priest and a monk of the Order of Saint Francis of Assisi, escorted by troops, rushed from house to house, urging on the carnage and seeking for those who were in hiding. The mountains echoed with the crumbling of ruins, with the fall of avalanches and rocks, and living bodies.

Children left orphans, and lost in the woods, or torn from the poor relics of their families, were carried away, like lambs to the butcher, to be educated in convents and monasteries in the faith of the murderers of their parents.

Léger, the historian, who with the hero Janavel had opposed the reception of the crusaders into the homes of their people, visited all the places of the massacre after it was accomplished, and wrote down from the mouths of the persecuted their individual experiences. "Let no one say that I have exaggerated these horrors," he says, "on account of what I have myself suffered. What shall I say? My God, the pen falls from my hands!" The heart recoils from repeating the terrible account he gives of what he saw and heard. The lovely valley of Luserna seemed a burning furnace, where cries that daily grew fainter attested that a martyr people once lived there. All of these noble and courageous sufferers might have saved their lives by abjuring their faith. Many continued firm in the prisons of Turin and Villafranca ten and twenty years after, forgotten by all but God.

Numerous apostates who had yielded to fear and despair dragged on miserable lives, bearing a heavy burden of shame and remorse. Two of these unhappy men — far more unhappy because they had been pastors — were forced by the Jesuits, their masters, to visit in prison Michelin of Bobi, who had suffered horrible mutilations and tortures, and remained firm in the faith, notwithstanding the torments of mind and body to which he was still subjected. Their dreadful duty was to persuade the old man to abjure, as they had done. They afterwards returned to the fold, touched, perhaps, by the awful surprise of Michelin, when he heard their object in coming, which caused his death.

James and David Prins of Villar suffered intense torments in the prison of Luserna, without yielding their religious opinions. These were two of six brothers who had married six sisters, forming one large patriarchal family, the eldest brother and sister acting as heads. This family consisted of more than forty persons living together in harmony, all of whom had their appointed tasks in the house, the vineyards, and the fields. Scenes like this, of touching Christian simplicity and love were converted by this persecution, — known ever after as the "Easter of 1655," — into a desert.

Accumulated horrors appalled the inhabitants, and greatly reduced their numbers.

This massacre, prepared in cold blood, and with horrible premeditation, was followed, thirty-one years later, by another, which resulted in the total exile for three years and a half of the Waldensian people.

# CHAPTER XII

### THE "GLORIOUS RETURN" IN 1689

THE glorious return of the Waldenses to their homes in the Piedmontese valleys was an episode in the great war which, in 1689, convulsed the continent of Europe. Led by the pastor-hero Henri Arnaud, who acted on the counsels of Joshua Janavel, they availed themselves of a fortunate moment, when both of their persecutors, Louis XIV. and Victor Amedeus II., were occupied elsewhere to escape from their kind entertainers in Switzerland. Three years and a half before, Louis XIV., "le Grand Monarque," to satisfy an uneasy conscience, became the champion of the Papacy, persecuted the French Protestants by revoking the Edict of Nantes, and urged the Duke of Savoy to drive out the Waldenses from Piedmont, threatening to send fourteen thousand French soldiers into the valleys, and reducing him to the alternative of seeing his kingdom invaded by

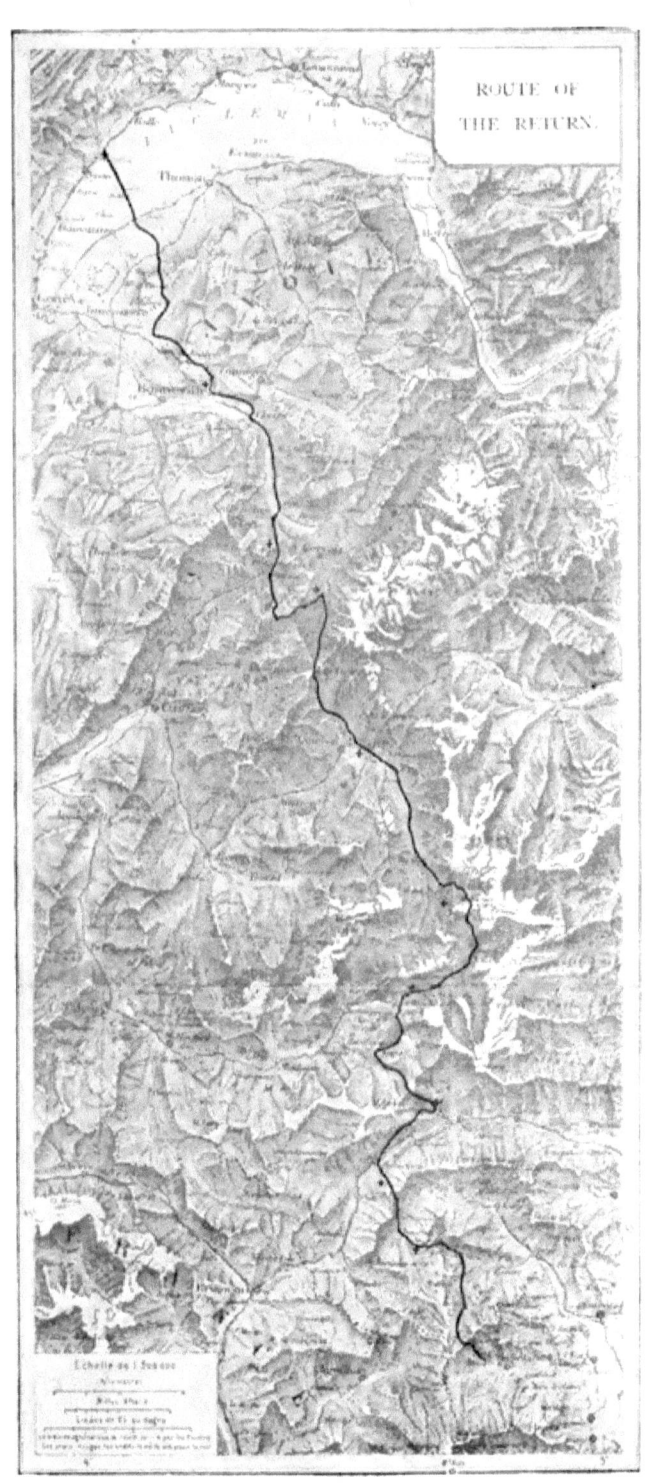

foreigners, or of persecuting the heretics himself.

Victor Amedeus II. preferred the latter, and ordered the Waldenses to cease the exercise of their religion immediately and forever. Every religious meeting was prohibited on pain of loss of life and property; all ancient privileges were abolished; the churches must be demolished; pastors and teachers must embrace the Catholic faith or leave the country within fifteen days; and children must be given within eight days after birth to the curates, on pain for the mother of being publicly whipped, and for the father of five years in the galleys.

This was war to the knife.

"O messa, o morte," — "Go to mass or you die." Three times the victims sent humble supplications for mercy to Turin, but received no answer, for their sovereign, placed between two fires, refused to listen to their cry, and soon began the persecution, notwithstanding the prayers in their behalf, made by Protestants of Germany, Holland, and England. On Good Friday of 1686, when the people were gathered in the church of Angrogna, Pastor Arnaud prayed, "Lord Jesus! Thou who hast suffered and died for us, give us grace to suffer and die for Thee. He who is faithful to the end shall be saved." Then all said together, "I can do all things through Christ, who strengtheneth me." The Lord's table at Easter was so crowded that the commemoration was held in the open air, and for many it was the last time.

The fatal order was given on April 22, 1686, and in one month the valleys were depopulated. Two armies, the French under General Catinat, and the Piedmontese under Gabriel of Savoy, moved in concert against this martyr people. Some were burned alive, some flayed, some hung to the trees, some thrown from precipices, some used as targets for the soldiers. Forty-two men and a few women and children retired to the heights of one mountain, and an equal number to another, where they dwelt in caves and fed on wild herbs and the meat of wolves. But the remainder of the population, about twelve thousand — thirteen thousand having been killed — were driven like cattle to the prisons of Turin, thirty miles distant. Four thousand babies were torn from their mothers' arms, and dispersed in convents or Catholic families. Five hundred adults were presented to Louis XIV. for the galleys at Marseilles.

CATINAT.

## The "Glorious Return" in 1689

Eight thousand died in the prisons of Turin, where they were heaped one upon another, fed on black bread and foul water, and made to sleep on the bare bricks, on the earth or wet straw, eaten up by vermin and left all night without a light, even when the sick were dying. They were melted by the heat in summer and frozen by the cold in winter, while the priests and nuns sought by every infamous means to convert them.

When the order came, obtained by the entreaties of the faithful Swiss, to liberate the survivors and send them over the mountains, although it was in the depth of winter, to a refuge in Switzerland, all were impatient to leave those terrible prisons.

Weak and sick, they prepared to leave at night, dressed as they were, in rags. The order was read to them at five o'clock on a winter evening, and they walked ten or twelve miles that night, leaving behind, on their way, the dying and the dead.

The valleys were left desolate, the churches destroyed, the houses burned, the mountains strewn with corpses.

"Heresy is extirpated; there are no more Waldenses in the valleys; their religion and their name are forever proscribed in

Italy!" cried the Pope and Louis XIV. of France.

Three thousand five hundred Waldenses took the way of exile with no hope of ever seeing again their beloved valleys, and yet, three years and a half later, they returned with joy, singing: "The Lord hath done great things for us, whereof we are glad."

Three thousand reached Switzerland, but they were walking skeletons, weary, footsore, famished, and half clothed. They were received with a transport of pity, love, admiration, and generosity. Shoes were given them immediately; five thousand yards of linen, and as many of woollen stuffs were soon made into garments, and they were taken joyfully to the homes of their friends. But, notwithstanding all this kindness, the exiles pined for their own land, and made two unsuccessful efforts to return before that of 1689.

By the treaty with the Duke of Savoy, Switzerland promised to detain the exiles even by force, and prevent their return to Piedmont. Many were sent on to Wurtemberg, to Magdeburg, to the Grisons, and to the Palatinate. Those who went to the last-named country suffered in the religious war,

HENRI ARNAUD.

and returned to Switzerland more miserable, if possible, than before.

All must be done in secret, and the Waldenses would never have accomplished their return without the aid and direction of the two remarkable men, Joshua Janavel and Henri Arnaud.

Joshua was a soldier and native of the valleys in 1655, who had been banished to Switzerland. Too old to take an active part in the heroic return, he yet merits a chief place in its history. He was the soul of the enterprise, and for the part he took in it was afterwards expelled by the Swiss from Geneva. Together with Arnaud, in secret, he studied the route they should take and the means of passing through a hostile country. He knew all the mountain passes, and counselled the taking of hostages, perfect union among themselves, special care of their leaders, and, above all, constant prayer and faith in God. This was all he could do; but his Christian heroism was so well known that these counsels were obeyed.

Pastor Arnaud — barbe as well as leader — was forty years old. Before attempting the perilous return, he visited William of Orange, who encouraged him, and supplied him with money, well pleased to aid an enemy of Louis XIV.

Too long would be the story of the passage by night of the nine hundred warriors over Lake Leman, and the ten days of fatigue, war, and pain on the mountains of Savoy. They reached, at last, the borders of their valleys, and in the first town took down the door of a church to make a pulpit outside for Arnaud to preach from.

Driven back by the soldiers of the Duke of Savoy to Balsille, they defended themselves on that mountain all the winter, and found there a crop of ungathered corn, covered by a merciful Providence until then by the snow. Aided by the fogs and winds and rains and snows, which, a French officer said, "seemed to be at their command," they resisted for months the attacks of an army of fifteen thousand or twenty thousand men. Retreating from their barricades, fighting inch by inch, and at last driven to the very summit of Balsille, hope seemed lost.

But one of their captains led them, aided as usual by a fog, which hid them from their enemies, along the edge of a precipice. Escaped from that snare, they saw nothing before them but to wander from one moun-

VICTOR AMEDEUS II. DUKE OF SAVOY AND
PRINCE OF PIEDMONT.

From an engraving by De l'Amerssini. Published in Paris, 1684

tain to another, until all had left their bones in the snow.

But a great deliverance awaited them, and that very day they heard the wonderful tidings that Victor Amedeus had joined the league of their friend, William of Orange.

The siege of Balsille excited the wonder of Napoleon I., who considered it one of the greatest military deeds in history. Yet it is regarded with indifference by the thirty million inhabitants of Italy, few of whom have heard of it or know the glorious history of the Waldenses.

They returned to their beloved valleys, and with joy remembered the Psalm, — "If it had not been the Lord who was on our side, now may Israel say . . . when men rose up against us then they had swallowed us up quick, when their wrath was kindled against us."

# CHAPTER XIII

### EXTIRPATION OF THE COLONY IN CALABRIA

More than two centuries before the persecution in Calabria, a colony of Waldenses left the valleys of Piedmont, and settled on those fertile slopes of the Apennines in southern Italy. In the year 1340 two young Waldensian farmers were overheard at a tavern by the Marquis of Spinello of Calabria, expressing their desire to emigrate from the valleys of Piedmont, which had become too small for the growing population, the fields not yielding sufficient for their wants. "My friends," said the stranger, "if you will come with me I can give you rich fields in exchange for your rocks in a country where there is more land than there are laborers to till it." This was the beginning of the colony that flourished and grew rich in Calabria, and was finally destroyed by the murder of nearly all its members.

## Extirpation of Calabrian Colony

The two young farmers were sent, like Caleb and Joshua, to spy out the land; and on their report that it abounded in all kinds of fruit trees, in olives, and vines, chestnut, walnut, and oak trees, the emigration was decided upon.

Young couples were hastily married, but the joy of the new alliances was clouded by the anguish of separation from the friends left behind.

Houses and lands were sold, and the emigrants set out for their new home, carrying the Bible with them, as the ancient Israelites carried the ark of the covenant, and transplanting their laborious habits and pure morals to the other extremity of Italy. The entire population of the valleys accompanied them to the foot of their mountains, the aged fathers and mothers tearfully embracing, for the last time, those dear ones who would probably never return, and praying the God of their fathers to bless them in their distant homes.

Silently the emigrants departed over the green plain of Piedmont, and after twenty-five days of fatiguing travel reached Calabria. Their hearts often turned longingly to the valleys; but they had with them familiar objects, dear friends, and that trust in God which is worth more than native land.

Towns had grown up around them, to which they gave the names of those in Piedmont familiar to their childhood, and the colony became rich and prosperous.

The Marquis of Spinello and other proprietors rented them land at a low rate, which they cultivated according to their own ideas. They were granted the right to unite themselves in independent communities, to elect their own civil and ecclesiastical rulers, and to levy taxes without giving account to any one. This was liberty almost unknown at that period, and they knew well its value, for they drew up a kind of charter of these rights, which was confirmed by the King of Naples, then Ferdinand of Aragon. Their neat and prosperous towns, Borgo d'Oltramontani, San Sisto, San Vincenzo, and seven others presented a striking contrast to the filth and misery of the Roman Catholic villages near them. For the first time in Italy the Waldenses made this contrast evident which is seen wherever Protestants and Roman Catholics live side by side. The Marquis of Spinello, impressed by their wealth and prosperity, offered them on his land the site of another

# Extirpation of Calabrian Colony 97

town, and authorized them to protect it with walls. This town, called La Guardia, was afterwards the centre of the persecution.

The colony was increased at the end of the fourteenth century by the persecuted brethren of Provence, who settled in Le Puglie, on the borders of Calabria. Emigrants from all the Waldensian colonies were thus gathered in the south of Italy. They were visited regularly by the barbes, who came every two years to maintain their faith pure, and to keep them in remembrance of the mother country in Piedmont. Until the Reformation, these Christians lived in peace, not going to mass, or worshipping images, or having their children baptized by the priests, and were protected in their faith by their landlords. Landlords and priests were both persuaded by the large rents and tithes they gave to look over their heretical doctrines, until the general persecutions that followed the Reformation reached Calabria.

The excuses made for them by their landlords, that they were charitable to the poor, just in their dealings, and fearing God, no longer served, then, to protect them from the terrors of Rome.

Aroused by the example of their brethren

in the valleys, and following the counsel of the German Reformers, they bravely resolved to openly assert their existence as an Evangelical church, and asked the Synod to send them a fixed pastor. Full of this religious zeal, they did not heed the prudent counsels of Barbe Gilles, who, on his last visit, advised them to temporize and secretly arrange their affairs so that they could retire to the valleys on the approach of the storm. A few did so and were saved; but the rest, loth to leave their pleasant homes and the comparative wealth, which in two centuries had accumulated, for the poverty of the valleys, remained, and were annihilated.

The pastor sent to them was John Louis Pascal, a young soldier, born a Roman Catholic, in Cuneo, of Piedmont, who had been converted, and studied theology at Geneva.

Two days before he was chosen by the Synod for the mission in Calabria, he became affianced to Camilla Guarini, like himself a refugee from Piedmont at Geneva. The poor girl, on hearing his destination, said, weeping, "Alas! so far from me — so near to Rome."

They parted, never to meet again on earth; but the letters of Pascal to her from Calabria and from his prisons in Cosenza and Rome

## Extirpation of Calabrian Colony

are models of Christian love, patience, and heroism.

His zeal and courage in Calabria soon drew upon him the wrath of the priesthood. He was kept a prisoner seven months in the house of the Marquis of Spinello, two months at Cosenza, and after a cruel journey to Rome was imprisoned there six months in the dungeon of the Torre di Nona, only to issue from it to his trial at the convent of Minerva, and the day following to his death in the square of Castel Sant' Angelo. Before the Pope and cardinals he proclaimed his faith, calling the Pope Anti-Christ, and making them wish "that he were dumb, or the people who heard him deaf."

He was strangled, his body burned, and the ashes thrown into the Tiber.

The martyrdom of Pascal at Rome, and of his companions, Stephen Negrin and Mark Uscegli, who died from famine and torture in the prison of Cosenza, drew the attention of the Roman Inquisition to the Evangelical churches of Calabria.

The chief Inquisitor, Cardinal Alexandrini, who was present at the martyrdom of Pascal, went to Calabria, and employed all the usual arts of treachery to betray the Protestants.

First, at San Sisto, then at La Guardia, and afterwards, one by one, in all the Waldensian towns except those of Le Puglie, from which the inhabitants escaped to Piedmont, the people were betrayed, deceived, tortured, imprisoned, flayed alive, decapitated, or burned to death. Their corpses, entire or in fragments, lined the roads from Montalto for thirty-six miles, and the air was pestilential. Even the Roman Catholics were seized with horror, and an eye-witness of the murder of eighty-eight persons in La Guardia has left a thrilling description of the scene. "I can liken these executions," he says, "only to a butchery. The executioners led out the victims one by one, wrapped a cloth about the head, made them kneel down in a place outside, and then cut off their heads with a knife. The same bloody cloth served to bind the eyes of all. I leave you to imagine this spectacle. I am yet weeping at the remembrance of it. The meekness and patience of those heretics was extraordinary. All of the old died calmly; only the young betrayed some terror. I tremble with horror when I remember the executioner with the bloody knife between his teeth and the dripping towel in his hand, who entered the house and brought out the victims one by one to martyrdom and death, just as sheep are killed at the slaughter-house."

Words fail to describe the tortures of these persecuted ones. Women were burned to death, men were thrown from towers, — every torture was applied; some were covered with pitch and sulphur before being burned. The colony was destroyed; none remained to tell the tale except the few miserable apostates and a remnant who made their way through unexampled perils and fatigues to Piedmont. But the memory yet remains at La Guardia. The half-ruined church, with part of the word "Evangelica" on its front, is there, and the people — descendants of apostates — show where the blood ran down the hill in that infamous massacre.

When Signor Pons, the Waldensian pastor at Naples, a few years since, visited them, and spoke to them in the Waldensian dialect, which they still retain, they gathered around him in the street, and some wept as they said to him: "Why have our people so long deserted us?"

# CHAPTER XIV

### LANGUAGE CHANGED AFTER THE PEST IN 1630

THE language of the Waldenses was violently changed, in the year 1630, from Italian to French, after the pest, which deprived them of all their barbes but two, and carried off two-thirds of the population of the valleys.

They accepted the language of the Swiss pastors sent to their aid from Geneva, as they understood French, from their situation on the borders of France, and their relations with Evangelical brethren in the Val Louise, the Val Cluson, and the Val Pragela.

French was used in their churches and families from that time forward, and is even yet as familiar to them as the Italian. But their language before the pest, and that now used in all their schools and colleges was and is Italian, and their missionary preachers established in all parts of the peninsula, speak the purest Tuscan, learned at the theological college in Florence.

The pest, which thus introduced a foreign language into the pulpits of the valleys, was preceded by two years of unexampled misfortunes. Terrible storms on the mountains, and inundations of entire villages, cold winds which destroyed the last hope of the chestnut harvest, and unusual rains that ruined the grapes, reduced these poor Christians to poverty. The elements seemed preparing the way for that dreadful scourge which soon after swept over the valleys.

The pastors, fifteen in number, met in September, 1629, in fraternal union, for the last time on earth. Famine threatened the land, and they were constantly harassed by priests and friars. A French army, sent by Cardinal Richelieu, under the command of three marshals of France, invaded Piedmont, carrying the pest with it. Soon there were deaths in the valley of Perosa, and before long every town, hamlet, and farmhouse in Luserna and San Martino was filled with the dying and the dead. The pastors recommended to the afflicted people prayer, repentance, conversion, and would have ordered a general fast if the unsettled state of the country had not forbidden it.

Luserna and Perosa were continually

troubled by the passage of large armies between France and Piedmont, bringing with them the contagion. The pest broke out in May, and in less than a month one hundred persons had died.

Pastor Gros of Saint John, and Pastor Bernard of Perosa, each fifty years of age, died at the same hour, near sunset, on July 10th. Bernardin Jajuet, forty years old, pastor of San Martino, died on the twelfth of the same month. On the 19th the pastors of the valley of Luserna met in the church of La Torre, and gave Pastor Appie of Angrogna charge of the church of Saint John, vacant by the death of Joseph Gros. But the very next day Pastor Appie was seized with the disease, and died in four days, at the age of forty-five. Seven more pastors, and many of the principal laymen died in the month of August. These pastors were James and Barnabas Gay, father and son, the one sixty years of age, and the other twenty-eight; John Bruneral of Rora, aged forty-three; Laurens Joli, forty-five; Joseph Chanforan, fifty-six; John Vignaux of Villar, fifty-eight, and David Javel, fifty. The surviving pastors met on the heights of the mountain of Angrogna, near Pramol, on account of its distance from infected places, and its vicinity to the three valleys, to divide the charge of the desolated churches; and Daniel Rozel of Bobi was sent to Geneva to ask help from the ministers there, and conduct young Samuel Gilles, son of the pastor of La Torre, as a student of theology. But these messengers, one thirty, and the other nineteen years of age, were both stricken with the malady during the month of September, and before they had set out upon their journey. At the beginning of October, besides Minister Bonjour, who was an invalid and had retired after fifty years' service, there were only three pastors left, one for each valley. These were Valère Gros for Saint Martin, John Barthelemi for Perosa, and Peter Gilles for Luserna.

They met at Angrogna with twenty-five lay delegates to divide again the care of the churches and make another appeal for pastoral aid to their brethren in Dauphiny and Switzerland. But the scourge had not yet done its work, for one of these three remaining pastors, who seemed to have been spared by a special Providence to represent the afflicted valleys, John Barthelemi, died at the age of thirty-two. Anthony Léger was then recalled from Constantinople, where he had been acting as minister to the ambassador of the Low Countries, and Monsieur Brunet came from Geneva, while the pest was still raging, bearing the assurance that in the spring other Swiss ministers would follow him.

Peter Gilles of Luserna at last, with the exception of Valère Gros, remained alone, of all the pastors of the valleys, having lost his four eldest sons from the pest. But God gave him strength to bear this accumulated burden of grief and of labor. He went to all the parishes, preaching twice or three times on Sunday, and at least once every day of the week, visiting the sick and consoling the afflicted. Calm and courageous in the midst of the dying, he communicated to them his own unshaken confidence in God. "I passed," he says, "in the midst of the afflicted villages, which everywhere showed signs of death and mourning. *Ubique luctus, ubique pavor et plurima mortis imago*" ("Grief and fear everywhere, and many images of death"). This is the only Latin quotation in all his numerous writings, at a period when other writers constantly used them. The people thronged to his preaching in the open fields, which seemed to them safer from infection than the churches, and "were filled with praise and thanksgiving at the marvellous help their Heavenly Father gave them in the midst of such distress." The heat of the summer that year was extraordinary. The army of Richelieu pillaged houses and towns, and there were conflicts between the soldiers and the inhabitants. Before La Torre was invaded by the pestilence the generals and officers of the French army retreated there for safety, and to have the services of some good physicians and apothecaries. This also increased the woes of the inhabitants, and gave more victims to the disease when it broke out there. Rent, food, and medicines became very dear; the sick were not cared for; many of the dead were not buried; the fruits of the trees fell to the ground, and lay rotting there ungathered; the fields were not harvested, and the mills even were so infected that the people were afraid to use them.

Public affairs were in disorder, as all the men in authority were dead, as well as nearly all the surgeons and apothecaries. One or two of the surviving physicians, who Gilles is careful to say were not natives of the valleys, asked exorbitant prices for the simplest services. The interment of the dead cost so much that many before dying gave all their possessions for the promise of burial, and houses containing several corpses were burned down, as the easiest way of disposing of them.

Many houses and farms were abandoned, owing to the death of owners and cultivators. The highways were filled with dead bodies, and the breath of the desert seemed to have passed over all the towns, once so active and happy. Famine, pestilence, and war all together afflicted the Waldenses, and not even then were they free from the persecutions of the priests.

Twelve thousand inhabitants of the valleys died, and a great uncounted number of strangers who had retreated to these high regions for refuge.

At the close of the following year, when the pest ceased, the survivors began to reorganize their affairs, and put their houses in order.

At La Torre alone fifty families were extinct. Many large families were reduced to two or three persons; children were left without parents, and parents without children. An extraordinary number of marriages followed; the orphans were adopted by those bereft of their own children, and the churches were reorganized. "The History of the

Waldenses," by Peter Gilles, in two volumes, written with charming simplicity and truth, is a guide to all historians up to the year 1643. He began to write it before the pest, in Italian, but changed it to French after the Swiss pastors introduced that language.

The preface to his work, written when he was seventy-two years old, is addressed to all the pastors, elders, deacons, and members of the churches in the valleys of Piedmont and the neighboring valleys. "You know," he writes, "in part, how and by whom I was charged to collect the history of our churches, and with what care I have done it. I now present it to you, not in our common Italian language, as I began it, but in this, for the reason already known."

This fact of the sudden change of language from Italian to French, is confirmed by a later historian, Alexis Muston, who says, "Although the Italian language had been used until the arrival of the Swiss pastors in the preaching and teaching of the Waldenses, the French was then substituted, and Gilles translated his work, already begun in Italian, into French. From this period date the relations between the churches of the valleys and Geneva."

Thus is refuted the reproach often made to the Waldenses in their missionary efforts in Italy since 1848, — that they are French and not native Italians.

More than once, with Piedmont, they passed, by conquest, for a time, under French rule; but they are and always have been strictly Italian in sentiment, and also in language, except from the consequences of the pest in 1630.

# CHAPTER XV

### HEROES

EVEN in a nation of heroes like the Waldenses, some names stand out more conspicuously than the rest. These are Janavel, Jahier, and Arnaud, whose deeds rival those of any modern heroes. Janavel and Jahier, in 1655, defied the troops of Pianezza, and, with a few men, defended the mountain passes against large armies. With six against six hundred, Janavel, then known only as the Captain of the Vineyards of Luserna, protected his native town, Rora, and drove back the enemy without revealing the smallness of his own force. With sixteen men, six armed with guns and ten with slings, he repulsed the second attack, made by a battalion of the enemy. The vigor and intrepidity of his pursuit struck terror into the hearts of the enemy, who fled towards Luserna, without knowing the number of the Waldenses, nor how many of their own they left dead behind. Years after, in old age and exile, at Geneva, Janavel said, "We were few, but the stones from the slings of those ten boys, too young to carry guns, were effective on the retreating enemy." When a third attack, with superior force, was made on Rora, Janavel witnessed, at a distance, the burning and sacking of the town, and then, with an ardent prayer to the God of armies, led his little troop of seventeen men to a place where he almost destroyed the enemy, embarrassed as they were by the booty, and the flocks and herds taken at Rora. Returning to the Pian Pra, — a level plain on the mountains, — Janavel, with his men, knelt on the grass and prayed, "O God, we bless Thee for our preservation. Protect us in these calamities and increase our faith." Ten thousand men, at last, were sent by Pianezza to destroy Rora, a village of fifty houses, and vanquish the heroic defender. Janavel's wife and daughters were taken prisoners; he was threatened with their death and his own if he should be taken. "I prefer the most cruel torments to abjuring my faith," he answered. "As to my wife and daughters, they know whether they are dear to me. But God alone is master of their lives, and if you kill their bodies He will save their souls." Janavel united with Captain

Jahier, a lion-like mountaineer, worthy to be his companion in these courageous deeds. Together they attacked the town of San Secondo, and taught the persecutors to fear them. They pushed hogsheads full of hay before them to the walls of the town, by which they were protected from the hail of balls, and set fire to faggots they had brought with them, making such a smoke that they were concealed from the enemy. In this attack they killed eleven hundred of the enemy, and lost only seven men. Fighting thus against superior numbers, crowded between a precipice and a regiment of enemies, throwing avalanches of stones on their persecutors, and always beginning a battle with prayer, the Waldenses fought all that year with Janavel at their head. He was shot through and through in one of these skirmishes, but, after six weeks, recovered, Jahier taking the command in his absence. The last advice he gave to Jahier as he was carried away fainting and bleeding was to do no more that day on account of the fatigue of the men, who had had nothing to eat until late. But Jahier was tempted by the promise of an easy victory into an ambush, and there lost his life, although no Greek or Roman hero ever sold it more dearly. He killed the traitor who had betrayed him, invoked the aid of God, threw himself on the cavalry of Savoy, killed three officers, and, after making terrible havoc around him, at last fell dying to the ground from his numerous wounds. "He showed," says Léger, "great zeal for God and the service of his country, and had the courage of a lion as well as the humility of a lamb, giving the glory of all his victories to God. He was versed in the sacred Scriptures, intelligent, accomplished, and only wanting in prudence to moderate his courage." On the same day the Waldenses thus lost the services of both Janavel and Jahier; but brave lieutenants remained, and many officers from other countries came to offer their services and sympathy to the oppressed people.

Janavel lived in exile after peace was restored, and aided Henri Arnaud to plan the "Glorious Return" from Switzerland to the valleys in 1689. Arnaud, although not a native of the valleys, had, long before accomplishing this wonderful military deed, united his fortunes with those of the Waldenses. The grandeur of his character appears in every act of that time. He knelt in the forest of Prangins on the banks of Lake Leman, invok-

PRANGINS, LAKE LEMAN.
From a print.

ing the blessing of God on the perilous expedition. He led the nine hundred heroes, after crossing the lake at its narrowest point, away from the chief roads in Savoy, to avoid the French troops sent to arrest their progress, remounting to the sources of the rivers, never approaching large towns, following the crests of the snowy mountains from precipice to precipice, and reaching at last the beloved land.

Arnaud, at the beginning of the expedition, was not its chosen leader, but only one of the three pastors who were to counsel the General Turrel. But Turrel, on the seventh day, was killed, after having shown that he had lost faith in the enterprise. Arnaud then became the chief, and his name, together with that of Janavel, who planned it, is now inseparably connected with the "Glorious Return."

Courage similar to this was shown by the men of Saluzzo, a colony of the Waldenses which was afterwards destroyed. Churches, called the "synagogues of heretics," in 1510, ten years before the Reformation in Germany, were destroyed, men were burned at the stake, and the rest of the population took refuge with their brethren in Luserna, where they remained as guests five years. Weary at length of trespassing on the hospitality of these poor mountaineers, the Vaudois of Saluzzo met in the valley of Rora, at night, descended into the valley of the Po, and took possession again of their homes. Five Vaudois only fell in this expedition, when they struck terror into the hearts of the despoilers of their homes and lands, drove them out by force of arms, and re-established the faith of their ancestors.

Their skill and courage in dispute was not less than their heroism in battle or their patience in exile. Three of the principal men of the valley of Perosa were ordered to go to Turin by the Duke of Savoy, in 1602, at the instigation of the Archbishop. On their arrival, they were told that the Duke, "having heard in what high esteem they were held in Perosa, wished them to embrace his religion, so that on their return they might influence others." The three heroes answered that "for the great affection they had for the Duke they would have yielded any point regarding the concerns of this world, but as to their religion, which they knew to be true, they would not leave it, and they prayed his Highness not to press them further on this point." At this response the Governor poured forth a torrent of abuse, threatening them with the indignation of his Highness and confiscation of their goods. Not long after, an order was published to all the inhabitants of Luserna and the vicinity to become Roman Catholics or leave the place in five days under pain of death and confiscation.

The Duke of Savoy himself was lenient, but, pressed by the Pope and the priests, was helpless to aid them. A new order was issued to those who had not left, to go in two days, unless they could obtain a special permission to remain from the Archbishop, which meant abjuration. Sure of their faith, but not ready with their Bible references, these poor people replied, "We cannot dispute with you, but if you send to our pastor and prove to him that the mass and your other ceremonies are not contrary to the Word of God, we will go to the mass." The Archbishop, believing himself sure of the victory, sent a safe-conduct to Pastor Augustus Gros, who, a convert to Protestantism, had been an Augustine monk at Villafranca. But Pastor Gros, remembering that no faith was to be kept with heretics, refused to accept it, and invited the Jesuit to Saint John. The conferences which were to convert the people to Papism began, at length, with the subject, "The mass was instituted by Jesus Christ, and is found in the sacred Scriptures."

Pastor Gros refuted all the arguments of the Jesuit, proved that the mass was nowhere mentioned in the Bible, and at last, to the confusion of his Jesuit adversary, said, "I promise to go myself to mass, and exhort my people to do the same if you will reduce it to the simple form in which the communion was instituted by Christ." These disputes were constantly held in all parts of the valleys, the pastors and teachers always putting the enemy to flight with argument, as the people did the armies with their slings and stones.

Some of these unfortunate mountaineers, so often disturbed, deprived of their goods, spirited away to far-off prisons and never more heard of, tortured in mind, body, and estate, and banished from their homes, gathered in a band in the mountains, and proclaimed themselves defenders of the oppressed. But as on the mountains there was no food, they were often obliged to make incursions to the plain, living by pillage, and creating reprehensible disorders. They were called the "Banished," and the "Digiunati," or "Fasters," and they constrained many of the apostate Protestants to return to their faith. This system of pillage, habitual with the Roman Catholics, was only once practised by the Protestants, except in legitimate defence of their homes, and it was then universally condemned.

Patient and uncomplaining, they often accepted exile and poverty as the least of the evils that encompassed them. Rather than accept the mass, which was worse than death, they "left their beautiful abodes, round which the vine hung its clustering fruit; left the shade of their chestnut groves, the hearths of their forefathers, the temples of their God, and, headed by their pastor, went forth, the mother with her children, the father bearing on his shoulders the household articles of most value and utility, unless, as was often the case, these were left behind, to take, instead, a more cherished freight, — some aged parent or helpless invalid."

# CHAPTER XVI

### MARTYRS

EVERY town and city of Piedmont has witnessed the martyrdom of some Waldensian. Every rock in the valleys is a monument of some death; every field has seen the martyrs tortured; every village has rendered its quota to the glorious phalanx, whose names are written in the Book of Life. Unheard-of tortures were invented for them, but their courage rose according to their need. The announcement of death was received as the entrance to life, and the martyr often bounded with joy on to the funeral pile that would soon reduce his mortal body to ashes. No books could be large enough to contain all of these touching stories, but some accounts of the later persecutions have been preserved. The barbe, Martin Gonin, of Angrogna, thirty-six years old, was sent by the Synod, in 1536, to Geneva, to confer with the Swiss pastors on ecclesiastical affairs. Returning

## Martyrs

through Dauphiny, he was arrested as a spy, there being war at that time between the King of France and the Duke of Savoy, and taken to Grenoble, where the Parliament recognized his innocence and ordered his liberation. But the jailer, having searched him in the night, found on his person some letters from Farel and other Protestants, and arrested him the next day on the new charge of heresy. He was examined regarding his faith, which he openly confessed, and was then condemned to be strangled and thrown into the Iser. This barbarous decree was executed at night, in order that his persuasive speech and gentle manners should not influence the spectators. Near the same time, Catelan Girardet, of San Giovanni, in Luserna, was condemned to the stake, which he endured with admirable fortitude. Before dying, he took two stones, and struck them together, saying, "You can no more, by your persecutions, destroy our Church than I can crush these stones with my hands." Twelve men of Luserna were at one time condemned to the stake, but were liberated by the people of Angrogna. At another time five together were burned alive, making a good confession of their faith. Sometimes the proposed victims, even when taken in the traps of their enemies, escaped, and spent long years of usefulness afterwards among their friends.

Pastor Gilles, returning from his last journey to Calabria, passed by Venice and Switzerland, taking with him from Lausanne a young man named Noël. In their inn they were accosted by some soldiers, who evidently suspected them of being heretics, and asked where they came from, where they were going, and why they were travelling thus together, a small weak man and a large robust one. Gilles answered that he was a Piedmontese, that he had been to exercise his profession in the kingdom of Naples, and that he was returning to Piedmont. He and Noël succeeded, with the aid of the tavern-keeper, in escaping that night, and, passing over by-roads in the woods and on the mountains, reached Luserna in safety. Many others held firm in the midst of tortures and at the hour of death. Even the judges sometimes implored the martyrs to save their lives by yielding, adding that they themselves desired a reform in the Church, but not out of it. But, like Saint Paul, the Waldenses boldly preached Christ and Him crucified, and often drew tears from the eyes of those who condemned them to an awful death. This serene strength of soul, superior to the ancient Stoicism, upheld them at the supreme hour. They accepted martyrdom like any other service for God. "Lord God, Father Eternal and Omnipotent, we confess, before Thy divine majesty, that we are miserable sinners, incapable of any good. Have pity upon us, Holy God, Father of Mercy, and pardon our sins, for the love of Jesus Christ, Thy Son, our only Redeemer." This prayer, so often on the lips of dying martyrs, is still used in the service of the Waldensians of the valleys as well as in those of Rome, Florence, Naples, Venice, Turin, Milan, and the other cities, where they now have churches.

Geoffray Varaglia, the son of one of the persecutors sent to the Waldensian valleys by Innocent VIII., became pastor of the very town that his father had laid waste. His story is one of the most touching in all the history of the Waldenses. He was born at the Piedmontese town of Busca, entered the Roman Catholic priesthood in 1522, and, having remarkable intelligence and great eloquence, attracted the attention of his superiors. He was selected to study and refute the doctrines of the Reformation, the same as those of the ancient Waldenses, which had taken new life at the Synod of Angrogna, when Farel and other reformers were present. With one companion and ten assistants, Varaglia was ordered to go over the cities of Italy to raise the credit of the Roman Church by his eloquent preaching. But these twelve men were all soon convinced of the truth of the doctrines they were called to refute, and were imprisoned in Rome five years, their new faith by this long seclusion growing daily stronger. When Varaglia was at length released, he attached himself to the legation of the Papacy in Paris; but the voice of conscience and the horror excited in his mind by the persecutions in Provence induced him to quit his lucrative position, and go to Geneva to study the new theology. At fifty years of age Varaglia began his pastorate at San Giovanni of Luserna, filled with an ardor that he had not felt in his youth. Returning from a visit to Busca, his native town, he was spied and taken prisoner to Turin, and, after trial and condemnation, led to the stake in the square of the castle of that city. When he heard the decree he said quietly to the judges, "Be sure, my lords, that you will need wood for the funeral piles sooner than Evangelical ministers to burn on them, for these increase in numbers day by day, and the word of God endures forever." After Varaglia had mounted the pile, the executioner approached and knelt before him, to ask forgiveness for putting him to death. "I pardon not only you," said the martyr, "but all the others who have caused it."

An old man, who had already suffered much for the truth, was led to Varaglia's place of martyrdom, and, after being made to witness it, was whipped, and then branded with red-hot irons heated at the fire which had reduced the strangled body of his friend to ashes.

Nicholas Sartoris, twenty-six years of age, a native of the valleys, who had studied at Lausanne, was present at Aosta when a priest said that the sacrifice of Christ was renewed every day in the mass. "Christ died but once," murmured Sartoris, "and is now in heaven." For this he was imprisoned, tortured, and at last burned at Aosta, May 4, 1557, courageously refusing to purchase life at the cost of abjuration. The cruelty of their enemies was sometimes foiled when everything was ready for the execution. Several of "the religion," condemned to death, were saved by a heavy fall of snow and rain, which prevented the wood from burning, and during the night were enabled to escape to their friends, glorifying God for their deliverance.

A pastor, named Jacob, who was bound to the stake with his mouth gagged so that he should not speak to the bystanders, so moved his judges by the expression of resignation and strength upon his countenance that one of them resolved never again to take part in such proceedings; and another, the Count of Racconis, from that time no longer a persecutor, sought in every way to befriend this afflicted people. The speechless death of this martyr was thus more useful to his friends than a victory on the battlefield.

The Abbey of Pinerolo, founded by the Countess Adelaide, of Morienne, in the year 606, was inhabited by rich monks, who were mortal enemies of the Protestants of the valley of Perosa, which touches Pinerolo. They hired about three hundred desperadoes, and sent them frequently into the valley to burn, destroy, and practise every kind of cruelty and brigandage on helpless men and women. These raids were often made upon the town of Saint Germain, only three miles distant, and the victims were dragged to Pinerolo, and imprisoned in the dungeons of the abbey until the judges found time to condemn them to fire or to the galleys. The pastor of Saint Germain, hearing one night a voice that he knew calling him, went out of his house, and found himself betrayed into the hands of these marauders, who had accompanied the traitor to make him prisoner. Several men of Saint Germain, who ran to his aid, were either killed, wounded, or taken prisoner; the houses were sacked, and the minister, together with some women, dragged to the abbey. The minister, after resisting all efforts to make him retract, was burned at a slow fire, the faggots of which were brought by the poor reluctant women, his parishioners. Preaching monks were often sent into towns to urge persecutions, and it is recorded that one of these, during a mild winter, proclaimed that God meant to save the wood so that more heretics might be burned.

The martyrs and sufferers were not all of humble condition, or even pastors and teachers. Many of the nobles of Luserna and of the plain of Piedmont accepted the pure religion of the Waldenses, and in times of persecution retired to the valleys for protection and sympathy. The noble family of Villanova Sollaro, consisting of six brothers, resisted all efforts to make them apostatize. "Let his Highness," said they, "ask of us any sacrifice but that of our faith;" but as the Duke of Savoy was determined not to have "two religions" in his kingdom, they hastily sold part of their possessions and retired into the marquisate of Saluzzo, then owned by France. The record of their five years of trouble and domestic agitation, always wandering between Saluzzo and Piedmont, has been preserved. They were at length cited to appear before the Senate of Turin with other persons of high degree, culpable, like them, of being Protestants — were condemned and banished, their wealth confiscated, and the members of the family dispersed. One of the brothers retired to the valley of Luserna, where his family existed for more than a century. The record of the martyrs might be continued, but this is enough to prove their courage, their patience, and humility.

Another list might be made of the unhappy apostates, who, to save their lives and fortunes, denied the convictions of their hearts, and dragged out for years miserable lives, leaving the inheritance of a false and cruel religion to their posterity. But the saintly courage of the martyrs was not possessed by all. Perhaps even on the families of the apostates a blessing rested, for the sake of ancient martyred ancestors, that afterwards blossomed in all Piedmont into the flower of Liberty.

# CHAPTER XVII

### WOMEN

MANY women courageously shared in the persecutions suffered by their people, and gave up their lives at the stake or on the wheel. Some noble ladies of Piedmont and Dauphiny openly professed the evangelical faith, and protected the oppressed, even at the loss of all their possessions. Others, of royal lineage or of noble birth, were distinguished for their cruelty and bigotry. The most conspicuous of these persecutors were Yolande, sister of Louis XI. of France, and wife of Amedeus IX., Duke of Savoy, who, in 1476, issued an edict ordering all the inhabitants of Pinerolo, Cavour, and Luserna to become Roman Catholics; and Maria Cristina of France, regent for her two sons, and generally called Madame Royale. In the persecution of 1655 this royal lady of the houses of France and of Savoy tried to prevent the remnant of the massacred population from taking refuge in the valleys of France after climbing the precipices and crossing the snow and ice of the mountains. She wrote to the court of France, urging Mazarin to send them back to her that they might be massacred, but he refused her tiger-like request, saying that humanity compelled him to give an asylum to the fugitive Waldenses. Marguerite de Foix, widow of the Marquis of Saluzzo, who was the slave of her confessor, became in his hands, in 1499, an instrument of persecution. Being a relative of Pope Julius II., she had a bishopric on her marquisate, and at the suggestion of the priests, by whom she was surrounded, issued a decree by which all the Protestants on her lands should leave or be put to death. She drove most of her unhappy subjects out; imprisoned, tortured, and killed those who remained, afterwards taking possession of their houses and lands. Most of the fugitives took refuge in the valley of Luserna in the towns of Angrogna, Rora, and Bobi, remaining there as guests five years, and sending frequent petitions to the Marchioness of Saluzzo for permission to return to their homes, all of which she refused. The situation became at length unbearable, and they took by force what was refused them in justice, losing only five men in the conflict.

In contrast to this, Blanche, widow of the Count of Luserna and lord of Angrogna, sympathized with her persecuted subjects in the invasion made by Commissioner Bersour, in the year 1535. She reproached him for the cruelties practised upon them, and for the want of respect to her and to the memory of her husband.

The saintly patience of the martyrs and of the tortured, brought to the castle where Bersour committed his cruelties, so moved the heart of one of his sons, Louis Bersour, and of his wife, Cristine Farine, that they became Protestants, and suffered great losses with the people of God. Their son, Paul Bersour, a learned and pious physician, lived in the valley of Luserna, and left a family which long preserved his name and that of their ancestor, the great persecutor of the church. Leonora, daughter of the Count of Luserna, and the wife of Valentine Boulle, who long faithfully resisted the persuasions and threats of the Duke of Savoy, was not less resolute than her husband in attachment to the religion she had adopted. Subjected to continual annoyances, they at last retired to Bobi, hoping there to escape further persecution.

The Protestant Countesses of Luserna often, in times of severe persecution, used their influence to protect the persecuted, — or, if Papists, tried to persuade them to abandon their religion, and thus save their lives and fortunes. But the best friend they had among these titled women was Marguerite of Valois, sister of Henry II. of France, and wife of Emanuel Philibert, Duke of Savoy. She had learned to admire the Protestant religion from her paternal aunt, Margaret of Navarre, and also from her maternal aunt, Renée, Duchess of Este, daughter of Louis XII. of France, both of whom were Protestants.

Like them, she protected the persecuted when she could, but the persistence of the Pope, priests, and friars was such that she was powerless to help them when the Duke was obliged to issue an edict of persecution. One of the touching epistles directed to her by the pastors of the little Alpine flock is preserved by the historian, Gilles. "Your Grace," it says, "is not ignorant of the beautiful examples of those good women, Deborah, Esther, and Judith, who, in positions like yours, spared not their own lives, and the Lord did great things for them in delivering his poor people, and gave them great glory and honor not only on earth but in heaven. Madame, this good God calls you to receive the honors of these women. Will you permit the Lord Jesus to be driven from your kingdom, and that the land where you live and have so much power should be bathed in his blood before your eyes?" The long letter of which this is a part is signed by "The poor and humble subjects, the inhabitants of the valleys of Luserna, Angrogna, Perosa, and San Martino, and all those of the plain who invoke only the name of the Lord Jesus." During all her reign as wife of Emanuel Philibert, she presented their petitions to the Duke, received their deputations, sympathized with them in their sufferings, and when they were imprisoned sent them food from her own table.

Pastor Noël, who was sent to the court to obtain her intercession, writes thus of her to his brethren, the ministers of Luserna: "I have seen Madame the Princess, and thanked her for all the pain and labor she takes for us, and for the favors that she, through God, has obtained for us. I cannot tell you of all the kindness and affection this virtuous lady has shown us." Some of her letters to her "Dear and well-beloved friends" are preserved, and prove the care she had for their interests, and her respect for liberty of conscience, which, she said, "no one ought to offend." She was deceived by the cruel Governor Castrocaro, whom she placed over her faithful Waldenses, believing his specious promises of kindness to them. But they never lost confidence in her, and lamented her death, which occurred in the year 1574. She continually exhorted the churches to obey Castrocaro, and they, for the "great love which they bore to their sovereign lady and princess, who had so often befriended them," tried to please her, but suffered much from his persecutions.

History recounts the martyrdom of many women of the Piedmontese Alps. Some were buried alive; some left wounded and starving to die on the snow; some were cut to pieces, and others put to death in modes too horrible to describe. Camilla Guarini, the very day that she was affianced to John Louis Pascal, heard that he was appointed missionary pastor to Calabria. It is uncertain whether they married at Lausanne, previous to his departure, but she never saw him again, and her heart was broken with grief for the tortures he suffered at Cosenza, at Naples, at Rome in the Torre di Nona, and finally at the stake in Castel Sant' Angelo. The letters he wrote to her at that time are models of affection and courageous faith and hope. Another martyr, before his fiery death, wrote to "Anne, his faithful spouse, and well-beloved sister," praying her to remain true to the faith she had adopted. "If the world and poverty affright thy youth," he says, "marry again some other man who fears God, and remember me only as a handful of dust. Trust in God. Pray to Him, love Him and serve Him, and He will never forsake thee." Jeanne Mathurin of Carignano asked leave of the persecutors to visit her husband in prison, as she had something to say to him "for his good." She was permitted to enter, the Inquisitors believing that she intended to persuade him to recant. But this courageous daughter of the martyrs, fearing that her husband might, from weakness or affection for her, fail at the last hour, earnestly exhorted him to persevere in his religion, and not weigh the short life of this mortal body against his eternal salvation. She was fiercely insulted by the priests, who were transported with fury at hearing language so different from what they had anticipated, and, refusing to retract, she also was kept prisoner, and was burned at the stake with her husband three days after. "God be thanked," said this heroic young woman to her husband, "He united us on earth, and He will not separate us in death. We shall meet in Heaven." One of the most touching stories is that of Octavia Sollaro, the daughter of one of the six brothers of the noble family of the Sollaro, who, to escape persecution in the plain of Piedmont, took refuge in the valley of Luserna. After long hesitation, she consented to marry a rich and noble lord of Piedmont, who promised to respect her religion. But he proved faithless to his word, denied her liberty to make any public profession of her faith, and deprived her of the Bible and other religious books. Octavia Sollaro, although restored to the wealth and titles of her ancestors, pined away, from this constant friction with the will of her husband and from the reproaches of her own conscience. When some good women of the valleys went to visit her, and "hoped that God would soon restore her to health," she answered, sadly, "No, do not ask God for that, but pray rather with me, that He will take me out of this life while I yet love his truth, and while the little light that remains to me is mine," and soon after died. Gilles, who relates this story in few and austere words, adds, "I tell this, so that others may profit by it on similar occasions." The wife of a man who, in conversation with some Papists, said "he thanked God that the Duke was more moderate and merciful than they" — because when he refused to recant they imprisoned him — went to Turin, threw herself at the feet of the Duke, explained her husband's words as a compliment instead of a reproach, and saved him from the jaws of the lion. Sometimes man and wife who were more nearly related than the papal Church arbitrarily allowed, were separated, the husband sent to the galleys, and the wife publicly whipped. A woman who was accused of preaching, "dressed in a great black robe," was put five times to "the question," in presence of the clerical and civil authorities of the place. Two beautiful girls were stolen — taken in a carriage to Turin, and never heard of more. Maidens threw themselves from precipices to escape dishonor; mothers pierced their own bosoms with a sword, and then handed the weapon to their daughters with a smile, and "It does not hurt." The granddaughter of a man one hundred and three years old gave him milk in times of starvation in the caverns, from her own breast, and, when he was killed before her eyes, leaped off a rock to escape the ruffians.

When their husbands and fathers and friends and lovers were fighting, the women retired to the caverns on the mountain heights to pray. The victory was often given in answer to their prayers. But once these women heard their friends from the valley of Cluson, who had come to aid, returning discouraged from the battles, say, "What will you do, poor women? Your husbands are all dead."

Margaret, the sister of the hero, Janavel, received a shot in her bosom when nursing her infant, and was killed soon after by a second shot. The babe was found three days after, alive, in her stiffened embrace. She was one of one hundred and ninety-six persons killed in their retreats in the mountain caverns at the time of Pianezza's invasion. The bones of these heroic women whitened "on the Alpine mountains cold," but they wear the martyr's crown of glory, and their stories are left to touch every noble and sympathetic heart.

# CHAPTER XVIII

### FRIENDS — GENERAL BECKWITH

MANY persons in the ranks of their enemies were struck with horror at the persecutions suffered by the Waldenses, and defended their cause with such earnestness that they themselves fell under the ban of Rome. A doctor of theology, who had signed many of the processes which condemned the so-called heretics to death, declared, "before God, that he had no peace of conscience since," and was driven from the assembly, and pronounced "more worthy of the flames than many who had been condemned to them."

Cardinal Sadoleto, who was friendly to the French Vaudois living near his possessions in Provence, was called to Rome, where he died shortly after, "quite suddenly, after receiving the sacrament." The Dukes of Savoy, although all Roman Catholics, except the excellent Margaret of France, were often reluctant to persecute their subjects living in the valleys. To the disgrace of womanhood, two women of the House of Savoy are known to have persecuted with vigor, — Yolande of France, and Cristina, called Madame Royale, — both regents during the minority of their sons. It is recorded of Carlo Emanuel, in 1595, that he received the inhabitants of Luserna in Villar, and in answer to their expressions of fidelity said, "Be faithful to me, and I will be a good prince and father to you, and as to your liberty of conscience and the exercise of your religion, I will do nothing against them. If any one disturbs you come to me and I will protect you."

Victor Amedeus II., in the next century, after being forced by the Pope and the King of France to persecute them, visited their desolate land, and comforted them with kind promises. The scene is famous in which he took the gold chain from his neck to divide among the starving peasants of the valleys. The sympathy of the people of Switzerland was shown by acts of abounding generosity. Geneva is a name that to this day wakes a thrill of grateful emotion in the heart of a Waldensian. Cromwell was moved to the depths of his strong heart by the news of the massacre of 1655. He ordered a general fast, gave two thousand pounds for the survivors, and wrote letters of remonstrance to the Duke of Savoy and to Louis XIV. The English Ambassador, Sir Samuel Morland, who had received the horrible details from Léger, one of the persecuted, addressed the young Duke in Latin, his bigoted mother being present. Horrified by the accounts he had heard, Morland relates them all in the very court of the Duke. His blood boils with indignation, and he says, "The angels are surprised with horror! Heaven itself seems to be astonished at the cries of dying men, and the very earth to blush with the blood of so many innocent persons." He then delivered a letter, also in Latin, composed by Milton, from Oliver Cromwell to the Duke, interceding for the Waldenses. Cromwell threatened the Pope to appear with English ships at the port of Civita Vecchia, near Rome, if the massacres were continued.

The famous sonnet of John Milton —

"Avenge, O Lord, thy slaughtered saints, whose bones
Lie whitening on the Alpine mountains cold"

was written at this time. The Elector of Saxony also remonstrated with another Duke of Savoy for these cruelties practised on the men of the valleys of Italy. "Let your Highness know that there is a God in Heaven from whom nothing is hid. Let your Highness take care not voluntarily to make war upon God, and not to persecute Christ in the person of his members. The ashes of the martyrs are the seed of the Church. The Christian religion was established by persuasion, not by violence." The "Glorious Return," in 1689, signalized the end of bloody persecution, but not of oppression and disabilities for the Waldenses. They lived over a hundred years, shut up in the valleys in poverty and ignorance, their ancient faith almost forgotten. Still the race was kept entire by the edicts of 1698 and 1730, which banished all persons of foreign birth, and by the interdiction of mixed marriages. In the year 1825 a religious revival began to prepare the way for that exodus which took place in 1848. A young French officer of artillery, named Félix Neff, dedicated himself to evangelization, first in the high Alps of Dauphiny, and afterwards in the Piedmontese Alps. But the work was difficult, as he said that the inhabitants had degenerated morally as well as physically. Many of the Waldenses, without having openly changed their religion, were farther from the faith of their fathers than if they had become Roman Catholics.

The sublime and terrible aspect of the French Alps, which served as a refuge for the truth when nearly all the rest of the world lay in darkness, — the deep caverns where the Protestants met in secret to read the Holy Scriptures, and adore the Eternal One in spirit and in truth, impressed the soul of this Evangelist. The year after, when he visited the Italian Alps, he was equally impressed with the natural scenery. "The beauty of the vegetation in these valleys contrasts with the aridity of the French Alps. The view of these rocks and glaciers, the rich valleys stretching away beneath your feet, and in the distance the vast plains of Italy, lift the thoughts to the Eternal Creator." The spiritual character of Félix Neff influenced the inhabitants of the Italian valleys. Prayer meetings were held, and Christian zeal awoke that showed itself in good works.

This awakening at home produced new interest abroad in the children of the martyrs. The Ambassador of Prussia collected money from the Czar, Alexander I. of Russia; from the Protestants in Rome, Turin, Genoa; in Holland, England, Prussia, Switzerland, the

## Friends — General Beckwith 145

Low Countries, and the United States, to build a hospital at La Torre. The hearts of the long-persecuted and neglected Waldenses overflowed with tenderness.

"This is the Lord's doing, and it is marvellous in our eyes," they said. "How many reasons we have to bless the Lord and to redouble our efforts to merit such kindness." A few years later another hospital was founded in Val San Martino. Another friend came to Italy in 1823, — the Rev. Dr. Gilly of England, — whose book, "Narrative of an excursion to the mountains of Piedmont and researches among the Waldenses, — Protestant inhabitants of the Cottian Alps," aroused widespread interest in the subject, and inspired one generous heart to give five thousand pounds sterling for the establishment of Trinity College at La Torre. The reading of this book also procured for the Waldenses the most generous, the most enlightened, and the most persevering of all their benefactors, General Charles Beckwith, whose benefits to the ancient Church of the Waldenses can scarcely be exaggerated. It would be difficult to find another example of a rich and cultured gentleman, in high position, who has left his country to live with a poor and rough population of Alpine peasantry, and for nearly one quarter of a century spent almost all of his income, his time, strength, and talents for their material and spiritual good. A cannon ball at the battle of Waterloo took off the leg of Beckwith, who was then an aide-de-camp of the Duke of Wellington, and constrained him to retire from active service at the age of twenty-six. The courage and energy which had made him conspicuous in the army were thenceforth all directed to the aid of the small, lifeless Church which, for the sake of the fathers, God meant to revive.

"Beckwith possessed all the best qualities to command an army: promptness in devising plans; coolness in danger; talent for organization and indomitable courage." But the French ball at Waterloo cut off all his high hopes of glory, and he was led to the Waldensian valleys. "I was transported," he said, "by the love of glory, but the good God said to me, 'Halt!' and cut my leg off, and I think I am much happier for it."

Since the emancipation of the Waldenses, many friends in Scotland, England, and other Protestant countries have aided their missions in Italy by sympathy and contributions. But none have collected as large sums, or aided as much in many ways as the Rev. Robert Stewart, of Scotland, but who lived over thirty years in Italy. A mural tablet in his honor, with an appropriate inscription, is placed in the entrance of the Waldensian Church, 107 Via Nazionale, in Rome.

## CHAPTER XIX

### EMANCIPATION IN 1848

THE hour of liberation from the woes of centuries at last arrived. The religious awakening in the valleys, fostered by General Beckwith, prepared the way for the emancipation from all their disabilities granted by Charles Albert of the House of Savoy. Long before the European revolutions of 1848 this noble-hearted king had begun to loose the fetters of his subjects. He softened the rigor of ancient edicts by special decrees, and in February, 1848, granted a liberal constitution, and emancipated the Waldenses. As Grand Master of the order of Saints Maurice and Lazarus, Charles Albert, in 1844, went to La Torre to assist at the dedication of a Roman Catholic church in honor of those saints. Although this seemed an unfortunate event, the benevolence of the sovereign and the fidelity of the inhabitants of La Torre made it the seal of affection and friendship between them. The King sent back the troops that were ready to accompany him and were to be lodged at La Torre, saying, "I have no need of a guard among the Waldenses." He then accepted the proposal of the Marquis of Luserna and the Marquis of Angrogna to be received by the militia of the valleys. In silence he passed through their ranks to the new church at the entrance of the town, and on his return was greeted by cries of joy and welcome from all the population. Moved by this cordial reception, the King, from the door of a palace at Luserna, reviewed all the Vaudois companies, saluted every banner of the different towns, and smiled when an enthusiastic color-bearer, not content with saluting the flag, also took off his cap. He received the *Tavola*, or Board of the Pastors, with distinguished honor, and left a gift for the poor. On his way back to Turin he saw bonfires, like a circle of fire, burning on the topmost peaks of the mountains, in token of the joy his visit had caused. "I shall never forget," said Charles Albert, "these tokens of affection, for they have shown in the hearts of these Waldenses the same devotion to the throne of Savoy which distinguished their ancestors." He erected at the entrance of La Torre, in memory of this visit, a small fountain, with the inscription, "The King Charles Albert to the people who welcomed him with so much affection in 1844."

The decoration of the order of Saints Maurice and Lazarus was afterwards sent to General Beckwith, — the man who had been called by a Roman Catholic bishop the "wooden-legged adventurer," and had been in danger several times of being expelled from the country on account of his efforts to educate the population. The darkness of the night of centuries gradually disappeared before the light. In 1847 Marquis Robert D'Azeglio headed a petition signed by six hundred other persons — professors, lawyers, doctors, notaries, artists, and even priests — for the civil and religious emancipation of the Waldenses and of the Jews. Public opinion in Piedmont was favorable to this progress of liberty. At a patriotic banquet given in Pinerolo, a lawyer said, "On these mountains live twenty thousand of our brothers, who are deprived of the rights of citizenship, and yet they are as educated, as industrious, as strong in arm and in heart as any other Italians. It is our duty, as their nearest neighbors, to lift our voices in their favor, and cry, 'Viva the Emancipation of the Waldenses.'" A similar banquet was soon after held at Turin, when all present joined in this cry of liberty and fraternity.

The Statute, or constitutional charter, was granted by Charles Albert on the 8th of February, 1848. But although the Waldenses participated in the general enthusiasm, they were as yet only tolerated, the ancient edicts against them being still in force. Eight days after, towards evening, when it was known that the decree of their emancipation was signed, thousands of the people of Turin gathered under the windows of Pastor Bert's house, and sang there a patriotic hymn, continuing these demonstrations of sympathy far into the night. The edict, which noted "the fidelity and good sentiments of the Waldensian population," granted them "all the civil and political rights of other subjects, with liberty to frequent the schools and universities, and to take all academic honors." Their religion and their private schools were ordered to be respected, notwithstanding any previous law against them. This edict created great joy as soon as it was known in the valleys. At La Torre there was a general illumination in the evening; and next day, called by the beating of the drums, nearly all the people gathered, every company with its banner, in and about the temple where Pastor Meille celebrated divine service. The hymns of joy sung in chorus, the solemn gratitude of the people, the banners gathered in the church, proved it a memorable occasion. All day long, companies of the national guard marched through the town singing patriotic songs like —

> "Con l'azzura cocarda sul petto,
> Con Italici palpiti in cuore,"

and crying, "Viva l' Italia," "Viva la Costituzione," "Viva Carlo Alberto."

Messengers were sent to all the mountain towns and hamlets, and that night more than one hundred fires on the heights were counted from La Torre. At Pinerolo, that centre of papal intolerance, from which, during many centuries, bands of priests and friars and persecutors of every sort had often gone out to La Torre, eight miles away, not only the few Waldenses who lived there, but all of the Roman Catholic population illuminated their houses for joy that a new era of peace and brotherly love had come. At San Giovanni

## Emancipation in 1848

the prior not only illuminated his house, but had the chimes in the belfry ring the most lively melodies. The national guards went out in the country near San Giovanni to bear the glad tidings to Joshua Meille, the venerable senior of the pastors. This good old white-haired man went weeping from one to the other, embracing all the young men, and saying, "Viva la fratellanza." But all this was nothing to the celebration at Turin on Feb. 28. The deputation from the valleys set out the day before, and was greeted all along the thirty miles of the journey by cries of "Long live our Waldensian brothers and liberty of conscience." By the time they reached Turin their number had increased to several hundreds, all of whom were joyfully received and lodged by the Turinese. Some merchants even converted their stores into dormitories for them. Early next morning the deputation of six hundred, preceded by twelve young Waldensian girls, dressed in white, with blue sashes, and bearing small Italian flags in their hands, met to take part in the procession. They had a magnificent velvet standard, with the royal arms embroidered in silver, and the simple inscription, "The grateful Waldenses to Charles Albert."

Oppressed and persecuted as they had been, they expected only to follow at the end of that interminable procession, where thirty thousand flags bent before Charles Albert. But the Turinese made them go first. "You have so long been the last," they said, "now you shall go first"; and the flowers thrown from the balconies fell first on the white and blue robed girls, children of the martyrs.

The delegates were embraced with tears; their hands were pressed by strangers, and even priests threw their arms about them as they walked in the procession. Liberty and Brotherly Love were the watchwords of that day. It is impossible to describe the affection and enthusiasm of the time, as if the Turinese would make amends for all the sins of their ancestors and of the papal Church.

"Dear brother," said an eye-witness, "who would have thought that we should ever see such wonders? Who would have said that on that same square of the Castle, where once arose so many funeral piles for our martyrs, where crowds drew near to view their sufferings, a similar throng should welcome us with such heartfelt cries of love and brotherhood? Oh! it is God who has done this. To Him be glory and thanks. May He ever bless our beautiful country."

From that memorable day the Waldenses, no longer shut up in their valleys, have had full liberty in Italy to teach the Gospel of truth, which preserved them from destruction amid so many and great perils and sorrows. They carried with them the Bible, which had been their light through all, that sacred Book which their ancestors, in 1535, ten years after the Reformation, gave a large sum from their slender purses to have translated into French by Olivetan, a kinsman of Calvin. On the first page of this edition are the lines, "The Waldenses, an Evangelical people, have made this treasure public," and the frontispiece is — "The Bible, which is all the Holy Scripture, containing the Old Testament and the New, translated into French, the Old from the Hebrew and the New from the Greek. God is All. Listen ye Heavens, and thou, Earth, lend thine ear, for the Eternal speaketh."

# CHAPTER XX

A. D. 1889 — BI-CENTENARY OF "GLORIOUS RETURN"

THE Bi-centenary of the "Glorious Return," celebrated by the Waldenses in the year 1889, was an event that called the attention of all Italy. The valleys, where for three years, from 1686 to 1689, no Bible was read, no psalm sung, no prayer of their pure faith raised to God, rang with joyful hymns of praise. Pastors from every part of Italy met at the Synod held at Torre Pellice, the capital of the valleys. There also came representatives of the Huguenots of England and America, of the Moravians, and of the Evangelical churches of France, Sweden, Holland, and Austria. A monument in memory of the departure for their valleys in Piedmont of Arnaud's nine hundred heroes was dedicated at Prangins, on Lake Leman. The inscription on it is this: "After three years of sojourn in this hospitable land, the

SIEGE OF BALSIGLIA.
From an old print.

## Bi-centenary of "Glorious Return" 157

Waldenses of Piedmont started from this spot to return to their own land, Aug. 16, 1689. The children of those heroes have erected this monument Aug. 16, 1889." The morning ceremonies were followed by a banquet, when the Italian Consul to Switzerland compared this heroic deed to the struggle of the Italian nation for liberty, from the defeat of Novara to the breach of Porta Pia at Rome. With great applause was sent to King Humbert a telegram expressing the devotion of these descendants of the persecuted Waldenses to the liberal sovereign and faithful keeper of the promises made to their forefathers.

Towards evening a small company of courageous youths embarked on the placid waters of Lake Leman, at Nyon, the narrowest crossing, to follow for ten days, over the high mountains of Savoy, the path taken by their ancestors in far more difficult circumstances. On Aug. 27, three thousand people gathered on the mountain of Balsiglia, in the valley of San Martino, where, two hundred years before, the fugitives arrived, and were besieged for six months by the army of their enemies, the French, escaping only miraculously, under cover of a fog, by creeping along the narrow ledge of a precipice. On Sept. 1 there was another reunion at Sibaud, where, Sept. 1, 1689, the returned exiles swore to combat the Babylonian woe. In the year 1694 the edict of restoration of the Waldenses to their homes in the valleys, to freedom from bloody persecutions, and to liberty of conscience, called forth a fiery protest from Pope Innocent XII. But the Senate of Turin prohibited the publication of this bull, and thus gave their first resolute resistance to the papal power over the Waldenses. Thus was inaugurated the era of liberty of conscience, and this faithful people began at last to enjoy the longed-for rest from persecution. When will the other inhabitants of Italy understand that because they trusted in God they were delivered, and learn the same undoubting faith which saved them? Two hundred years ago these valleys were deserted, and the few heroes who came back from Switzerland were uncertain whether new exile and new persecutions awaited them. What a contrast to the liberty now enjoyed by their descendants! Benevolently considered by their fellow-citizens in the Italian peninsula; the bi-centenary of the "Glorious Return" treated as a national glory; reduced railroad fare granted them in their journey to the valleys, and the sympathy of the successor

WALDENSIAN RESIDENCE AND MUSEUM.

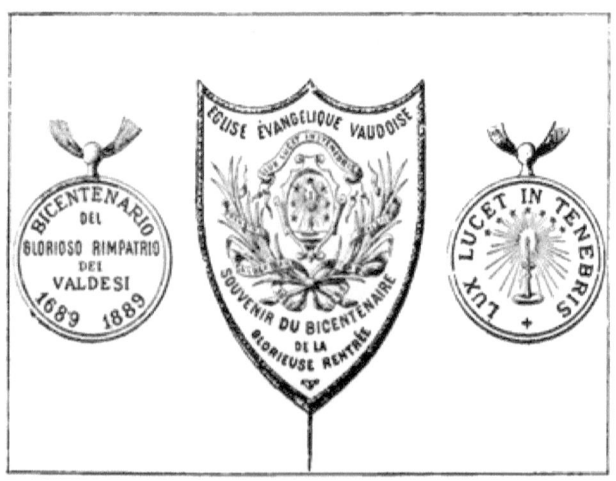

BADGES.

of their ancient persecutors, they are now satisfied. King Humbert gave also a contribution of five thousand francs to the Waldensian House and College, built by them in commemoration of the bi-centenary. He has also conferred the title of Commendatore of the Crown of Italy on two pastors — Dr. Lantaret, of the valleys, now deceased, and Dr. Matteo Prochet, President of the Committee of Evangelization; and of Cavaliere of the same order on several others, and decorated Dr. Paolo Geymonat, of Florence, with the title of Cavaliere of the Order of Saints Maurice and Lazarus. An eye-witness thus describes two visits of King Humbert to the valleys:

"In the year 1892 there was to be a sham fight of the troops in the Val San Martino, and the King was expected. Thousands of people were gathered on the hills and in the trees to witness his arrival, and a pavilion was erected at the place where he was to leave his carriage. First on the line to receive the King were one or two members of Parliament, then four priests and fifteen mayors, and at the end the Moderator of the Waldensian Church and the President of the Committee of Evangelization, the programme being that these were the last to be introduced. The

King arrived, alighted, shook hands with the deputies; then, perceiving the President of the Waldensian Committee, passed before priests and mayors without noticing them, and marched straight to him with outstretched hand, exclaiming, 'I am among friends. How do you do, Mr. Prochet?' So the first were last and the last first. The delight of the thousands of Waldenses, who saw their pastors so honored by their beloved sovereign, was unbounded.

"In the following year, 1893, the Synod being met at Torre Pellice, a deputation was sent to the King at Pinerolo. He received them in the most cordial manner, and in answer to the invitation to visit Torre Pellice, said that he was not sure that he would have time for it, but 'some time,' added he, with a smile, 'I shall come to see you.'

"The Synod closed; the members dispersed on Friday, and the following day the King, without warning any one, gave the unexpected order to his coachman to drive to Torre Pellice. Fortunately some one overheard the order and telegraphed to the Moderator. One hour elapsed between the departure from Pinerolo and the arrival at Torre Pellice of the royal carriage, and in that hour four thou-

# Bi-centenary of "Glorious Return" 161

sand people got the news, dressed in haste, and welcomed the King, who, alighting at the entrance of the town, walked between the Moderator and the Mayor, visiting successively the Casa Valdese, the church, and the hospital. When the people saw the King enter the church, which probably no prince of the house of Savoy had ever done before, their enthusiasm was indescribable.

"In the Casa Valdese the King read the inscription on the slab of marble, telling with grateful words of his gift, and, turning to the Moderator, said, 'Indeed, I did not deserve so much.' On leaving the town to return to Pinerolo he shook hands once more with the Moderator, saying, 'I loved your people before, but now I shall love them still more.'"

# INDEX

ABRAHAM, 37.
Adelaide, Countess, of Morienne, 126.
Adriatic, the, 9.
Aix, Bishop of, persecutes the Waldenses, 30.
Albi, the town of, 20.
Albigenses, the, unite with the Waldenses, 18; their name lost, 18; persecuted by Pope Innocent III., 19; their early history, 20; various names of, 20; origin of their name, 20; their numbers, 21; form to resist the tyranny of Rome, 21; their writings destroyed, 21; accused of Manicheism, 21; refuse to repent, 22; martyrdom of, 22; the Paulicians develop into, 24; possessed Peter Waldo's translation of the Scriptures, 39; contradictory accounts given of, 44.
Alexander I., Czar of Russia, gives money to the Waldenses, 144.
Alexandrini, Cardinal, the chief Inquisitor, 99.
Alpine Church, the, 59, 71.
Alpine valleys, the, 6, 9.
Alps, the, 2; guarded by the Waldenses against the inroads of Louis XIV., 4.
Alps of Dauphiny, the, 143.
Alps of France, the, Waldensian colony in, 63; exterminated, 63.
Ambrose, Bishop of Milan, "the Rock of the Church," 17.
Amedeus IX., Duke of Savoy, 63, 130.
Angrogna, Lord of, 132.
Angrogna, Marquis of, 149.
Angrogna, the mountains of, 66, 75, 104.
Angrogna, the Synod of, 124.
Angrogna, the town of, 51, 79; the Waldenses attacked in, 81, 87, 121.
Angrogna, the valley of, 49; synod held in, 63; invaded by the Inquisitors, 63, 74, 134.
Antichrist, the, 34.
Aosta, 125.
Apennines, the, 94.
"Apostolicals," the, see *Albigenses*.
Appie, Pastor, of Angrogna, death of, 104.
Apuglie, Waldensian colony in, 63; exterminated, 63.
Aquitaine, 8; the Albigenses in, 20.
Arles, Bishop of, persecutes the Waldenses, 30.
Armenia, 23, 39.

Arnaud, Col. Henri, the hero of the Waldensian return from exile, 9; on the origin of the Waldenses, 10; leads the Waldenses in their glorious return of 1689, 86, 87; plans to deliver the Waldenses out of Switzerland, 91, 114, 115, 156.
Asia, 24.
Avignon, Bishop of, persecutes the Waldenses, 30.
Azeglio, Marquis Robert d', heads a petition for the emancipation of the Waldenses, 150.

BAGNOLESE, the, 53.
Bagnolo, the Waldenses at, 53.
Balsiglia, the mountain of, 157.
Balsille, the town of, 92; the siege of, 93.
"Banished," the, 118.
Barbes, the Waldensian, 5, 40; meaning of the word, 55; the writings of, 56; their knowledge of the Bible, 57; location of their school, 57; their support, 57; their duties, 58; their language, 58; their annual synod, 59; their work, 60; generally unmarried, 61; as martyrs, 61, 62.
Barbets, 55.
Barcelona, church of, 8.
Baronius, Cesar, laments the corruption of the Roman Church, 61; submits to the Roman Church, 62.
Barthelemi, John, 105; death of, 105.
Bavaria, the Waldenses at, 54.
Beckwith, General Charles, the most generous of the benefactors of the Waldenses, 145; his benefits to the Waldensian Church, 145; his life among the Waldenses, 145; at Waterloo, 146; estimate of, 146; decorated, 150.
Believers, the, 21.
Bergamo, the Waldenses at, 53.
Bernard, Pastor, of Perosa, death of, 104.
Bernard, Saint, describes the Waldenses, 43.
Bersour, Commissioner, his invasion against the Waldenses, 132.
Bersour, Louis, becomes a Protestant, 132.
Bersour, Paul, 132.
Bert, Pastor, 151.
Bible, the, love of the Waldenses for, 2; Peter Waldo makes a translation of, 39; Olivetan makes a French translation of, 155.
Blanche, widow of the Count of Luserna, sympathizes with the Waldenses, 132.
Bobi, the town of, 51; the Protestant temple of, 72, 79, 131, 132.
Bohemia, 25.
Bonjour, Minister, 105.
Borgo d' Oltramontani, the town of, 96.
Botta, the historian, on Peter the Waldo, 29.
Bouillon, Godfrey of, takes Jerusalem from the Saracens, 37.
Boulle, Valentine, 132.
Brescia, the Waldenses at, 53.
Bricherasio, the town of, the Waldenses attacked in, 81.
Bruis, Peter de, 29.
Bruneral, Pastor John, of Rora, death of, 104.
Brunet, Monsieur, 106.
Bulgaria, 24.
Bulgarians, the, 20.
Busca, Waldensian colony at, 53; destroyed, 53, 123, 124.

# Index

CALABRIA, the Waldenses send a colony to, 53; destroyed, 53, 63, 94; the beginnings of the colony, 94; John Louis Pascal at, 98; the attention of the Roman Inquisition called to, 99; the people betrayed and killed, 100; the colony totally exterminated, 101.
Calvin, John, 29.
Cambridge, 34, 57.
Campanula Elatinus, the blue, 51.
Carlo Emanuel, promises to protect the Waldenses, 141.
Casa Valdese, the, 161.
Castel Sant' Angelo, the square of, at Rome, 99.
Castrocaro, Governor, placed over the Waldenses by Marguerite of Valois, 135; his treachery, 135.
Cathari, the, 20.
Catinat, General, marches against the Waldenses, 88.
Cattanée, Archdeacon Albert, tries to convert the Waldenses, 65; sends his army against the Waldenses, 65; meets with defeat, 66, 67; withdraws his army, 68.
Cavour, the rock of, 50, 77, 130.
Celibacy of the clergy, the, treatise written by Vigilantius Leo on, 8.
Cenis, Mount, 1, 48.
Chalance, the, 50.
Champforans, the Synod of, 61, 70.
Chanforan, Pastor Joseph, death of, 104.
Charlemagne, 13; at the Council of Frankfort, 16; the twelve counsellors of, 37.
Charles I. of Piedmont furnishes troops against the Waldenses, 64; withdraws his troops, 69; makes peace with the Waldenses, 69.
Charles Albert, King of Sardinia, gives a charter of liberty to the Waldenses, 46, 151; at La Torre, 148-150; gratitude of the Waldenses to, 153.
Charles Emanuel II., Duke of Savoy, 79.
Christ, the Jews the typical enemies and persecutors of, 37.
Christians, the, persecuted by the Jews and Saracens, 37; the Saracens the typical enemies and persecutors of, 37.
Cisalpine Gaul, Vigilantius retires from persecution to, 9.
Civita Vecchia, the port of, 142.
Claude, Bishop, enmity of Dungal to, 12; early life of, 13; his appointment as Bishop of Turin, 13; his work in Turin, 14; his writings, 15; his opposition to the adoration of the cross, 15; seals his faith by martyrdom, 16. See also *Seyssel, Claude*.
Clergy, the celibacy of, 8.
Cluson, the valley of, 139.
Coadjuteur, the, 59.
Col du Pis, the, 52.
Constance, the Council of, 78.
Constance, Queen, 22.
Constantine, Emperor, 8.
Constantine Sylvanus, founds the Paulicians, 23; ordered to be stoned, 23.
Constantinople, 105.
Cosenza, 98.
Cottian Alps, the valleys of, 1; the Waldenses in, 12; the ancient church of, 25; principal occupations of the inhabitants of, 45.
Cottius, King, 9.
Council of the barbes, the, 59.
Cowrnaout, the, 50.
Cristina, Maria, persecutes the Waldenses, 130, 141.
Cromwell, Oliver, sympathy shown for the Waldenses by, 141; intercedes for the Waldenses, 142.

Crusaders, the, 19.
Cuneo, Waldensian colony at, 53; destroyed, 53, 98.

DAUPHINY, the French province of, the Albigenses in, 20. 26, 48; the Waldenses attacked in, 68, 70, 105, 121.
"Digiunati," the, 118.
Dominic, the "blessed," canonized for his services, 19.
Dominicans, the, 30.
Dungal, his enmity to Bishop Claudio, 12, 16; his references to Vigilantius, 13.

EMANUEL PHILIBERT of Savoy, supplication of the Waldenses to, 10; grants amnesty to the Waldenses, 77; Marguerite of Valois the wife of, 133.
England, 87; contributes money to the Waldenses, 144.
Epistles, the, 57.
Erfurt, 27.
Este, Duchess of, see *Renée*.

FAREL, 70, 121.
Farine, Cristine, becomes a Protestant, 132.
"Fasters," the, 119.
Ferdinand of Aragon, King of Naples, confirms the charter for the colony at Calabria, 96.
Fleury, the Abbey of, 15.
Florence, Waldensian churches at, 1; the Waldenses at, 53; theological college at, 102.
Foix, Marguerite de, persecutes the Waldenses, 131.
Foucald, Bernard de, on the missionary zeal of the Waldenses, 60.
France, 20, 25.
France, King of, furnishes troops against the Waldenses, 64.

Francis I., of France, confession presented by the Waldenses to, 10.
Francis of Assisi, Saint, imposition of, 38.
Franciscans, the, 30.
Frankfort, the Council of, sustains Bishop Claude in his opposition to the worship of images, 16.
French, the, attack the Waldenses, 88.
French Alps, the, 37, 144.
French valleys, the, 52.
French Vaudois, the, 140.

GABRIEL of Savoy, marches against the Waldenses, 88.
Gascony, the Albigenses in, 20.
Gay, Pastor Barnabas, death of, 104.
Gay, Pastor James, death of, 104.
Geneva, 3; the library of, 57, 102, 105, 120, 141.
Genoa, Waldensian churches at, 1; the Waldenses in, 54.
Germanasca, the river, 49, 51.
German Reformation, the, 2, 54, 61; revives the faith of the Waldenses, 70.
German Reformer, the, 10; their friendship for the Waldenses, 54.
Germany, 25, 87.
Geymonat, Dr. Paolo, decorated by King Humbert, 159.
Gilles, Pierre, the historian of the Waldenses, 56; on the writings of the barbes, 55; on the confidence reposed in the barbes, 73; warns the colonists at Calabria to prepare for persecution, 98; at Luserna, 105; his burdens, 106; his "History of the Waldenses," 108, 109; escape of, 122; on the touching appeal of

# Index

the Alpine pastors to Marguerite of Valois, 133; on the fidelity of Octavia Sollaro, 138.
Gilles, Samuel, 105.
Gilly, Rev. Dr., of England, influence of his writings for the benefit of the Waldenses, 145.
Girardet, Catelan, of San Giovanni, 121; martyrdom of, 121.
"Glorious Return of 1689," the, 86; signalizes the end of the bloody persecution of the Waldenses, 143; the Bi-centenary of, 156–161.
Gnostic theology, 23.
"Good Men," the, see *Albigenses*.
Gregory IX., Pope, 19.
Grenoble, 121.
Grisons, the, 90.
Gros, Pastor Augustus, 117, 118.
Gros, Pastor Joseph, of Saint John, death of, 104.
Gros, Valère, 105, 106.
Gonin, Martin, of Angrogna, arrested as a spy, 121; ordered to be liberated, 121; arrested on the charge of heresy, 121; martyrdom of, 121.
Guarini, Camilla, affianced to John Louis Pascal, 98; Pascal's letters to, 98; her heart broken by Pascal's martyrdom, 135.

HENRICIANS, the, 20.
Henry II., of France, 133.
Henry, the Italian, 29.
Holland, 87; contributes money to the Waldenses, 144.
Holy See, the, 64.
Huguenots, the, 156.
Humbert, King, 4; the Waldenses express their devotion to, 157; his friendship for the Waldenses, 159; his two visits to the Waldensian valleys, 159–161.
"Humiliated," the, 30, 38.

INNOCENT III., Pope, persecutes the Albigenses, 19; condemns triclavianism, 38.
Innocent VIII., Pope, issues a bull of extermination against the Waldenses, 64, 123.
Innocent XII., Pope, makes a fiery protest against the Waldenses, 158.
Inquisition, the, 35.
Inquisitors, the, 19; their oppression of the Waldenses, 41; exterminate the Waldensian colony in Provence, 53; invade the valley of Angrogna, 63.
Iser, the river, 121.
Italian Alps, the, 144.
Italian language, the, 57.
Italy, 4.

JACOB, the pastor, martyrdom of 126.
Jahier, Captain, 111; attacks the town of San Secondo, 113; death of, 113.
Jajuet, Bernardin, pastor of San Martino, death of, 104.
Janavel, Joshua, the hero, 83, 86; plans to lead the Waldenses out of Switzerland, 91, 114; heroic acts of, 111; unites with Captain Jahier, 112; attacks the town of San Secondo, 113; wounded, 113; in exile, 114.
Janavel, Margaret, death of, 139.
Javel, Pastor David, death of, 104.
Jerome, charges brought by Vigilantius Leo against, 8; his violent answer, 9.
Jerusalem, 8; taken from the Saracens by Godfrey de Bouillon, 37.
Jesuitism, 78.
Jesuits, the, 84.

Jews, the, persecute the Christians, 37; the typical enemies and persecutors of Christ, 37.
John, Saint, the prophecies of, 33, 57.
Joli, Pastor Laurens, death of, 104.
Jonas of Orleans, on Bishop Claude's opposition to the adoration of the cross, 15.
Julius II., Pope, 131.

"LA BARCA," a Waldensian poem, 36.
La Chapelle, the town of, 52.
La Guardia, the town of, 97; the Waldenses massacred at, 100.
Languedoc, the Albigenses in, 20.
Lantaret, Dr., 159.
Latin language, the, 57.
La Torre, 104; invaded by the pestilence, 107, 108; hospital at, 145; Trinity College established at, 145; Charles Albert at, 148-150; rejoicing over the emancipation of the Waldenses at, 152.
La Tour, the capital of Luserna, 51.
Lausanne, 122, 125.
Lazarus, Saint, 148.
Léger, Pastor Anthony, on the Waldenses, 44, 57; on the massacre of the Waldenses in 1655, 83; recalled from Constantinople, 105; on Jahier's zeal, 114, 142.
Leman, Lake, 54, 92, 114, 156, 157.
Leo, the reputed founder of the Waldenses, 7; discredited by the Waldenses, 8. See also *Vigilantius Leo.*
"Leonists," the, 7; the "most pernicious sect of ancient heretics," 7. See also *Waldenses.*

Leonora, wife of Valentine Boulle, 132.
Le Puglie, the town of, 97.
Lombardy, the plain of, 53.
Louis XI., of France, 130.
Louis XII., of France, tribute to the Vaudois of, 44.
Louis XIV., of France, urges Victor Amedeus to persecute the Waldenses, 3; the Waldenses guard the Alps against the inroads, of, 4; becomes the champion of the Papacy, 86; revokes the Edict of Nantes, 86; thinks the Waldenses are exterminated, 89; Cromwell remonstrates with, 142.
Louis the Meek, 13.
Louis the Pious, 13.
Low Countries, the, 106; contribute money to the Waldenses, 145.
Lucifer, 21; the Waldenses accused of worshipping, 40.
Lucius II., Pope, condemns the Waldenses, 60.
Luserna, Count of, 132.
Luserna, the Countesses of, use their influence to protect the Waldenses, 133.
Luserna, Marquis of, 149.
Luserna, the valley of, 49, 50; the towns of, 51; the Waldenses in, 54; the barbes of, 71; the Waldenses massacred in, 84; the pest in, 103, 117, 121, 122, 128, 130, 131, 134.
Luther, Martin, the sudden religious impression received by, 27.
Lyons, the Archbishop of, persecutes Peter the Waldo, 29.
Lyons, 8, 25.

MAGDEBURG, 90.
Magi, the, at the cradle of the Saviour, 37.

# Index

Manicheans, the, 20.
Manicheism, the Albigenses accused of, 21; definition of, 21.
Man of Sin, the, 34.
Mantua, the Waldenses at, 53.
Margaret, Duchess of Savoy, gains clemency for the Waldenses, 77.
Margaret of Navarre, 133.
Margaret, Queen, 4.
Marguerite of Valois, her friendship for the Waldenses, 133; touching appeal of the Alpine pastors to, 133; Pastor Noël sent to obtain the intercession of, 134; deceived by Governor Castrocaro, 135.
Mariolatry, the doctrines of, 35.
Marseilles, the galleys at, 88.
Martel, Charles, conquers the Saracens, 37.
Martin, Henri, on the Waldenses, 45.
Mathias, the valley of, 52.
Mathurin, Jeanne, of Carignano, martyrdom of, 136, 137.
Maurice, Saint, 148.
Mazarin, 131.
Meane, the valley of, 52.
Meille, Pastor Joshua, 152, 153.
Messina, Waldensian churches at, 1.
Michelin of Bobi, 84.
Milan, Waldensian churches at, 1, 123.
Milton, John, 142.
Minerva, the convent of, 99.
Minor friars, the, 30.
Mission churches, Waldensian, money needed for, 5.
Monasticism, sanctity of, 8.
Mondovi, Noir de, leads the troops against the Waldenses, 66; his death, 67.
Monks, the, 55.
Montalto, 100.
Montfort, Simon de, 19.

Moravians, the, 156.
Morienne, 126.
Morland, Sir Samuel, 34; his indignation at the persecution of the Waldenses, 142.
Moslem, invasion, the, 16.
Mountaineers, the, 53.
Muston, Alexis, on the Waldenses, 45; on the Vatican, 47; Rome the cause of the Waldensian persecution, 79; on the change in the Waldensian language, 109.

NANTES, the Edict of, revoked by Louis XIV., 86.
Naples, Waldensian churches at, 1, 101, 123.
Naples, King of, see *Ferdinand of Aragon.*
Naples, Prince of, 4.
Napoleon I., 93.
Neff, Félix, dedicates himself to evangelization, 143; spiritual character of, 144.
Negrin, Stephen, the martyrdom of, 99.
"Noble Lesson," the, 6; the most ancient document of the Waldenses, 32; the spirit of, 32; the subject of, 32; doubt thrown on the antiquity of, 34; attributed to Peter Waldo, 34; proof of the antiquity of, 36, 38; on the contradictory accounts given of the Vaudois, 44.
Noël, Pastor, escape of, 122; sent to obtain the intercession of Marguerite of Valois, 134.
Novara, the defeat of, 157.
Nyon, 157.

OLIVETAN, translates the Bible into French, 155.
Order of Saint Francis of Assisi, the, 83.

Order of Saints Maurice and Lazarus, the, 148, 159.
Origen, the opinions of, 8.
Orleans, 15, 33.

PALATINATE, the, 90.
Palermo, Waldensian churches at, 1.
Papacy, the, believed by the Waldenses to be the predicted Anti-Christ, 33; Louis XIV. becomes the champion of, 86.
Papists, the, destroy Waldensian literature, 57; massacre the Waldenses at Torre Pellice, 80.
Paris, 124.
Paris, the Council of, sustains Bishop Claude in his opposition to the worship of images, 16.
Pascal, John Louis, burned at Rome, 53, 61; sent to Calabria, 98; affianced to Camilla Guarini, 98; his letters to her, 98; his zeal and courage, 99; his imprisonment, 99; his martyrdom, 99, 136.
Pastors, the Waldensian, 5.
Paterines, the, 20.
Paulicians, the, 20; converts from Manicheism, 23; founded by Constantine Sylvanus, 23; the principles of, 23; emigration of, 24; develop into the Albigenses, 24; possessed Peter Waldo's translation of the Scriptures, 39.
Pellice, the river, 49, 51.
"Perfect," the, 31, 38.
Perosa, the valley of, 49, 50, 51; the towns of, 52; the Waldenses in, 54; the pest in, 103, 105, 116, 126, 134.
Pest of 1630, the, 102–110.
Peter, Saint, the prophecies of, 33; Pope Innocent VIII. the pretended successor of, 64.

Peter the Waldo, of Lyons, 8; the founder of the ancient church of the Cottian Alps, 25; death of, 25; never recognized by the Waldenses as their head, 25; his various names, 26; his birth, 26; early education of, 26; crisis in the life of, 26; denounces the Roman Church, 27; devotes himself to missionary labors, 27; gives his property to the poor, 28; his separation from his family, 28; persecuted by the Archbishop of Lyons, 29; flees into Picardy, 29; his preaching, 30; his converts, 30; the "Noble Lesson" attributed to, 34; makes a translation of the Scriptures, 39.
Petrobrusians, the, 20.
Pianezza, Marquis of, a conspicuous persecutor of the Waldenses, 78; characteristics of, 78; his perfidious attack on the Waldenses, 80; defeats the Waldenses by treachery, 81–84.
Pian Pra, the, 112.
Picardy, 29.
Piedmont, 7; Peter the Waldo in, 29, 47; invaded by a French army, 103; martyrdom in, 120.
Piedmont, the plain of, 48, 49, 53, 63, 94, 127.
Piedmontese, the, attack the Waldenses, 88.
Piedmontese Alps, the, 135, 143.
Piedmontese Waldensian valleys, the, 54; glorious return of the Waldenses to, 86.
Pinerolo, 65, 69, 130, 150; rejoicing over the emancipation of the Waldenses at, 152, 160.
Pinerolo, the Abbey of, 126.
Planghère, Saguet de, 68.
Po, the valley of the, 116.

# Index

Pons, Signor, the Waldensian pastor, 101.
Poor Men of Lyons, the, disciples of Peter the Waldo, 29; persecuted by the Archbishop of Lyons, 29; later persecution of, 30, 38.
Porta Pia, breach of, at Rome, 157.
Pra del Tor, the school of the barbes at, 57, 59; the Count of Trinity tries to surprise, 75; the Waldensian victory, 75.
Pragela, the barbes of, 71.
Pramol, the town of, 104.
Prangins, 114; monument dedicated to the Waldensian heroes at, 156.
Preaching friars, the, 30.
Prins, David, 85.
Prins, James, 85.
Prochet, Dr. Matteo, 159, 160.
Propaganda, the Congregation of, motto of, 78.
Propaganda Fede, the College of the, established to persecute the Waldenses, 54.
Provence, the Albigenses in, 20; the Waldenses send a colony of farmers into, 52; exterminated by the Inquisitors, 53, 63, 97; persecution in, 124.
Prussia, contributes money to the Waldenses, 144.
Prussia, the Ambassador of, collects money for the Waldenses, 144.
Publicans, the, 20.
Puglie, the Waldenses send a colony to, 53; destroyed, 53.
Pyrenees, the, 8.

QUEYRAS, the valley of, 52.

RACCONIS, Count of, 126.
Raynouard, Mr., on the "Noble Lesson," 35.

Reformation, the, 2, 54.
Regidor, the, 59.
Reinerius, the Inquisitor, 31.
Renée, Duchess of Este, 133.
Revel, Pierre, of Angrogna, 67.
Rheims, 15.
Richelieu, Cardinal, 103.
Roman Church, the, its antagonism to the Waldenses, 1; the immoderate endowment of, 8; the idolatry and corruption of, 18; the Albigenses form to resist the tyranny of, 21; Peter Waldo denounces, 27; Cesar Baronius laments the corruption of, 61; he submits to, 62; Yolande orders the Waldenses to return to, 63.
Roman Inquisition, the, 99.
Romaunt languages, the ancient, 32, 34, 57.
Rome, Waldensian churches at, 1, 5, 6; the seven hills of, 34; to blame for the Waldensian persecution, 79, 98.
Rora, the town of, 51; burned by the Count of Trinity, 76, 79; heroically defended by Janavel, 111, 131.
Rora, the valley of, 49, 116.
Rorenco, prior of St. Rock, on the antiquity of the Waldenses, 12.
Rospart, the river, 51.
Royale, Madame, see *Cristina, Maria*.
Rozel, Daniel, of Bobi, 105.
Russia, Czar of, see *Alexander I*.

SACCO, Reinerius, an Inquisitor, on the "Leonists," 7.
Sadoleto, Cardinal, becomes a friend of the Waldenses, 140; his sudden death, 140.
Saint Germain, the town of, raids on, 126, 127.

Saint John, the heights of, 66; the Waldenses attacked on, 81, 117.
Saint Martin, 105.
Saint Remi, the library of, 15.
Saint Rock, 12.
Saluzzo, Marquis of, 131.
Saluzzo, Marchioness of, 131.
Saluzzo, Waldensian colony at, 51; destroyed, 53; the inhabitants take possession of their homes, 116.
Saluzzo, the marquisate of, 128.
San Giovanni, the heights of, 66; Varaglia at, 124; rejoicing over the emancipation of the Waldenses at, 152.
San Martino, the valley of, 49, 50, 51; the towns of, 52; the Waldenses in, 54; the Waldenses attacked in, 68; their victory, 69; the pest in, 103, 134.
San Secondo, the town of, attacked by Janavel and Jahier, 113.
San Sisto, the town of, 96; the Waldenses massacred at, 100.
San Vincenzo, the town of, 96.
Saracens, the, persecute the Christians, 37; conquered by Charles Martel, 37; Godfrey de Bouillon, takes Jerusalem from, 37; the typical enemies and persecutors of Christians, 37.
Sardinia, King of, see *Charles Albert*.
Sartoris, Nicholas, martyrdom of, 125.
Saviour, the, three Magi at the cradle of, 37.
Savoy, 115.
Savoy, Dukes and Duchesses of, bigotry of, 3; reluctant to persecute the Waldenses, 140.
Savoy, the mountains of, 54, 92.
Saxony, the Elector of, 142.
Scriptures, the, Peter Waldo makes a translation of, 39.

Seyssel, Claude, Archbishop of Turin on the origin of the Waldenses, 7. See also *Claudio, Bishop*.
Sibaud, oath taken by the Waldensians at, 5; reunion of the Waldenses at, 158.
Sicily, 1.
Simeon, converted, 23; becomes Constantine's successor, 24; burned, 24.
Sollaro, Octavia, marriage of, 137; her fidelity to her faith, 137; death of, 138.
Sollaro, Villanora, the noble family of, 128, 137.
"Song of Roland," the old Provençal, 36.
Spain, 8.
Spinello, Marquis of, 94; founds the colony at Calabria, 94, 96.
Spoleto, the Waldenses at, 53.
Stephen, 22.
Stewart, Rev. Robert, of Scotland, aid given the Waldensian missions by, 147; mural tablet in honor of, 147.
Stoicism, 123.
Subiasc, the river, 51.
Sweden, 156.
Swiss, the, 89.
Swiss pastors, the, 102, 120.
Switzerland, the Waldenses driven into, 4, 89; the Waldenses in, 54; the Waldenses escape from, 86; promises to detain the Waldenses, 90; sympathy shown the Waldenses by the people of, 141; contributes money to the Waldenses, 144.
Sylvester, Pope, 7; avarice of, 8.
Synod of the barbes, the, 59.

TAILLARET, the town of, burned by Pianezza, 82.
Tavola, the, 149.

# Index 173

Thirteen Lakes, the, plain of, 50.
Thrace, 24.
Tiber, the river, 99.
Torre di Nona, the dungeon of, at Rome, 99.
Torre Pellice, 73; Pianezza's perfidious attack on, 80; the synod held at, 156, 160.
Toulouse, 20.
Turin, Waldensian churches at, 1; "wholly given to idolatry," 14, 48; Geoffroy Varaglia burned at, 61, 82, 84, 87, 88, 89, 116, 124, 151; rejoicing over the emancipation of the Waldenses at, 153.
Turin, Archbishop of, see *Seyssel, Claude*, 7.
Turin, the Council of, urges Charles Emanuel II. against the Waldenses, 79; its decree against the Waldenses, 79; the Waldenses appeal to, 79.
Turin, the Senate of, 128; prohibits the publication of Pope Innocent XII's. bull against the Waldenses, 158.
Turinese, the, 153.
Turrel, General, death of, 115.
Triclavianism condemned by Pope Innocent III., 38.
Trinity College, established at La Torre, 145.
Trinity, Count of, attempts to defeat the Waldenses by treachery, 74; foiled, 74; tries to surprise Pra del Tor, 75; his defeat, 75; burns the town of Rora, 76; his army recalled, 77.
Trent, the Council of, recommendation of, 78.

ULTRAMONTANES, the, 60.
United States, the, contributes money to the Waldenses, 145.

Uscegli, Mark, the martyrdom, 99.

VAL CLUSONE, 52; synod at, 61, 102.
Valden, 26.
Valdenses of Piedmont, see *Waldenses*.
Valdensis, 26.
Valdensius, 26.
Val de Pragela, 52, 102.
Valdis, 26.
Valdius, 26.
Valdo, 26.
Vallenses, the, 53.
Val Louise, 44, 52, 68, 102.
Val Pellice, the valley of, 49.
Val Perosa, 52.
Val San Martino, hospital founded in, 145; sham fight at, 159.
Varaglia, Geoffroy, burned at Turin, 61; story of, 123, 125.
Vatican, the, 47.
Vaudois, the, evil meaning attached to the word, 41; contradictory accounts given of, 44; tribute of Louis XII. to, 44. See also *Waldenses*.
Vaudra, 26.
Vaulderie, evil meaning attached to the word, 41.
Venice, Waldensian churches at, 1; the Waldenses in, 54.
Vicenza, the Waldenses at, 53.
Victor Amedeus II., Duke of Savoy, the prince of the Waldenses, 3; drives the Waldenses into Switzerland, 4; loyalty of the Waldenses to, 4; orders the Waldenses to cease the exercise of their religion, 87; joins the league of William of Orange, 93; promises made to the Waldenses by, 141.
Victor Emanuel Ferdinand, Prince of Naples, 4.

Vigilantius Leo, the Leonist of Lyons, 8; work of, 8; his charges against Jerome, 8; Jerome's violent answer to, 9; retires to Cisalpine Gaul for safety from persecution, 9; references of Dungal to, 13.

Vignaux, Pastor John of Villar, death of, 104.

Villafranca, 84, 117.

Villar, the town of, 51, 73, 76, 79, 141.

Violante, see *Yolande*.

Viso, Mount, 1, 48; the "Jungfrau of the South," 49.

Vittoria, Waldensian churches at, 1.

WALDENSES, the Italian, location of, 1; their growth, 1; their churches, 1; persecution of, 2; refuse to recognize the Roman pontiff, 2; their love of the Bible, 2; never failed in patriotic love and service to their country, 3; driven into Switzerland by Victor Amedeus II., 4; guard the Alps against the inroads of Louis XIV., 4; the pariahs and outcasts of Italy, 4; restrictions of, 4; their lack of bitterness and revenge, 4; their fidelity to their oath, 5; their "barbes," 5; their mission churches, 5; their origin and traditions, 6; evidences of their early Christian origin, 6–9; meaning of the name, 8; confession presented to Francis I. by, 10; their supplication to Emanuel Philibert of Savoy, 10; refuse to be called a Reformed Church, 11; in the Cottian Alps, 12; Bishop Claude, 12–16; without a bishop, 16; extent of the influence of their church, 17; joined by the Albigenses, 18; never recognized Peter Waldo as their head, 25; the historian Botta on the name of, 29; marvellous growth of, 30; the "Noble Lesson" of, 32; believe the Papacy to be the predicted Antichrist, 33; a persecuted and suffering race, 40; accusations against, 40; oppressed by the Inquisitors, 41; the lovely modesty and humility of, 42; their converts, 43; described by Saint Bernard, 43; their contempt of death and suffering, 44; Léger on, 44; their principal occupations, 45; their type, 45; Muston and Henri Martin on, 45; Charles Albert, King of Sardinia, gives a charter of liberty to, 46; prohibitions of, 46; their location, 48, 49; send a colony of farmers into Provence, 52; send colonies to Calabria and the Puglie, 53; the missions of, 53; their friendship for the German reformers, 54; the College of the Propaganda Fede established to persecute, 54; their barbes, 55–62; their missionary zeal the cause of their persecution, 60; their thirty-three persecutions, 63; ordered by Yolande to return to the Roman Church, 63; Pope Innocent VIII. issues a bull of extermination against, 64; troops sent against, 64; their touching appeal, 65; their wonderful victories, 66-69; peace made by, 69; the German Reformation revives the faith of, 70; ordered to attend mass, 71; their response in arms, 72; attacked by the garrison of Villar, 73; their victory, 73; the Count

## Index

of Trinity fails in his treachery against, 74; their success against their enemies, 76; Emanuel Philibert grants amnesty to, 77; Margaret, Duchess of Savoy, gains clemency for, 77; the Marquis of Pianezza, a conspicuous persecutor of, 78; the Council of Turin urges Charles Emanuel II. against, 79; the decree against, 79; their appeal to the Council of Turin, 79; Pianezza's perfidious attack on Torre Pellice, 80; their escape to the heights, 80; attacked on all sides, 81; their successful defence, 81; deceived by Pianezza's treachery, 82–84; their glorious return in 1689, 86; escape from Switzerland, 86; ordered by Victor Amedeus II. to cease the exercise of their religion, 87; attacked by the French and the Piedmontese, 88; the exile into Switzerland, 89; their return from Switzerland, 91–93; their colony at Calabria exterminated, 100; their language violently changed, 102; the pest of 1630, 102; Italian in sentiment, 110; martyrs of, 120–129; persecuted by women, 130, 131; Bersour's invasion upon, 132; friendship of Marguerite of Valois for, 133; their touching appeal to, 133; Marguerite of Valois places Governor Castrocaro over, 135; the martyrdom of their women, 130–139; their friends, 140–147; Yolande's persecution of, 141; Madame Royale's persecution of, 141; Carlo Emanuel promises to protect, 141; value of Dr. Gilly's writings to, 145; Gen. Beckwith's devotion to, 145, 146; assistance given by Rev. Robert Stewart to, 147; the darkness of centuries gradually disappearing, 150; efforts made for the emancipation of, 150; constitutional charter of liberty granted to, 151; rejoicing over the emancipation of, 151–155; the Bi-centenary of their "glorious return," 156–161; monument dedicated at Prangins to the heroes of, 156; their reunion at Sibaud, 158; resolute resistance to the papal power over, 158; friendship of King Humbert for, 159.

Waldensian Church, the, extent of its influence, 17; ancient emblem of, 17; Peter Waldo the founder of, 25; the Apostolic origin of, 25; the Italian origin of, 25.

Waldensian House and College, the, 159.

Waldensian literature destroyed by the Papists, 57.

Waldensian manuscripts, 34.

Waldensian valleys of Italy, the, 26, 37; location of, 48.

Waldo, Peter, see *Peter the Waldo*.

William of Orange aids Arnaud for the Waldenses, 91; Victor Amedeus II. joins the league of, 93.

Women courageously share in the Waldensian persecutions, 130; their martyrdom in the Piedmontese Alps, 135–139.

Wurtemberg, 90.

YOLANDE orders the Waldenses to return to the Roman Church, 63; her persecution of the Waldenses, 130, 141.

www.ingramcontent.com/pod-product-compliance
Lightning Source LLC
Chambersburg PA
CBHW031827230426
43669CB00009B/1253